# The Everyday Samurai

# The Everyday Samurai

A

Modern Guide to

Living with

Intention and Honour

Adrian

Pengelly

© Adrian Pengelly 2023
First published 2023

All rights reserved. No part of this publication may be reproduced, stored in a retrieval system, or transmitted in any form or by any means, electronic, mechanical, photocopying, recording or otherwise, without the prior permission of the copyright owner.

The right of Adrian Pengelly to be identified as the author of this work has been asserted in accordance with the Copyright, Designs and Patents Act 1988

Author: Adrian Pengelly
Cover Design: iBUZZLink
Book Design: iBUZZLink
ISBN 979-8-38860-474-3

TheRogueHealer@aol.com
EquineHealer@aol.com

This book is not intended as a substitute for the medical advice of physicians or doctors. The reader should regularly consult a physician in matters relating to their health and particularly with respect to any symptoms that may require diagnosis or medical attention.

"Today's world is fraught with uncertainty and challenges, and it's easy to feel lost or overwhelmed. But by embracing the timeless principles of Bushido - honor, courage, compassion, respect, and loyalty - we can find our way forward. Whether in the boardroom, the dojo, or the battlefield of daily life, the samurai code offers a guide to ethical and effective action. With discipline, perseverance, and a commitment to self-improvement, we can become modern-day warriors, equipped to face any obstacle with grace and strength."

# Contents

| | |
|---|---|
| Introduction | 9 |
| Samurai Culture | 15 |
| The Sword | 21 |
| Wabi-Sabi and Kintsugi | 27 |
| Religion and Spirituality in Samurai Life | 31 |
| Training the Samurai | 49 |
| The Samurai in Pop Culture | 53 |
| Meet the Real Samurai? | 59 |
| The Samurai Women of Japan | 87 |
| Ronin Doctors and Sword Doctors | 93 |
| Origins of the Bushido Code | 99 |
| The Eight Virtues of Bushido | 109 |
| Becoming an Everyday Samurai | 133 |
| Rectitude | 141 |
| Courage | 151 |
| Benevolence | 161 |
| Respect | 171 |
| Honesty | 181 |
| Honour | 191 |
| Loyalty | 201 |
| Self-control | 213 |
| The Legacy of the Samurai | 223 |
| Conclusion | 231 |

# INTRODUCTION

**The Everyday Samurai is a book that transcends age, culture, and background. This book invites readers to reflect on their lives, values, and goals and take practical steps towards living a life of excellence. By embracing the principles of Bushido, readers can learn to live with purpose, meaning, and fulfilment and ultimately become the best versions of themselves**.

The samurai were a group of highly skilled warriors who lived in feudal Japan from the 12th to the 19th century. The samurai were more than just skilled warriors; they were a way of life in feudal Japan. These elite warriors lived by a strict code of ethics known as Bushido, which was deeply ingrained in their culture and influenced all aspects of their lives. Their adherence to this code made them renowned for their discipline, courage, honour, and loyalty, and their reputation still stands today as an epitome of excellence.

The samurai code of Bushido was based on eight core virtues: rectitude, courage, benevolence, respect, honesty, honour, loyalty and self-control. These values guided the samurai's behaviour, and they were expected to uphold them in every aspect of their lives, whether in battle or their interactions with others. Bushido was not just a set of rules to be followed but rather a way of being and thinking that required constant practice and self-improvement.

While the samurai era may be long gone, the principles and values of Bushido continue to resonate with many people today. The Everyday Samurai, a book that applies these ancient principles to modern life, offers readers a practical guide to living a life of purpose, meaning, and fulfilment. By adopting the samurai's values and mindset, readers can learn to cultivate discipline, face challenges with courage, show compassion and benevolence towards others, and ultimately live a life that reflects their deepest values.

In our fast-paced, modern world, losing sight of what truly matters in life is easy. We can become consumed by pursuing wealth, status, and success and forgetting the importance of honour, respect, and loyalty. By turning to the principles of Bushido, however, we can rediscover what it means to live a life of purpose and meaning. The Everyday Samurai provides practical advice on how to apply these principles to everyday life, from managing stress and anxiety to improving relationships and finding fulfilment in work.

The samurai were more than just warriors; they were exemplars of excellence in all areas of life. By adopting their values and mindset, we can learn to live with greater purpose, meaning, and fulfilment and ultimately become the best versions of ourselves.

The Everyday Samurai is a book that reminds us of the enduring relevance of the samurai code and offers a roadmap for living a life that is truly worth living. As we navigate through our busy lives, it's easy to get caught up in the daily grind of work, family obligations, and personal responsibilities. We often find ourselves feeling overwhelmed, stressed, and disconnected from the things that matter most. The Everyday Samurai aims to help readers reconnect with their inner strength and wisdom and to live their lives with intention and purpose.

The book is divided into twenty-two chapters, with eight focusing on a specific virtue of the samurai code. These virtues, when broken down, embody the universal principles of mindfulness, discipline, self-control, honour, courage, compassion, and wisdom. Each chapter provides practical advice and exercises to help readers develop these traits in their own lives. By the end of the book, readers will have a comprehensive understanding of how to live their lives according to the principles of Bushido.

The Everyday Samurai is more than just a book; it is a guide to living a life of purpose, meaning, and fulfilment. While the principles of Bushido originated in feudal Japan, they are not bound by time or place. They are universal and can be applied to any era, any culture, and any individual. The principles of Bushido are not just for warriors but for anyone seeking to live a life of excellence.

The Everyday Samurai is a book that reminds us of the enduring relevance of Bushido principles in the modern world. While we may not face the same challenges as the samurai of old, we still face challenges that require discipline, courage, and honour. Whether it is in our personal relationships, our professional lives, or in the face of adversity, the principles of Bushido can help guide us to make the right choices and live with purpose and meaning.

Regardless of where we are in life, The Everyday Samurai has something to offer us. As students, we can learn how to cultivate discipline, focus on our studies, and face academic challenges with courage and perseverance. As professionals, we can learn how to cultivate integrity and honesty in the workplace and navigate complex ethical dilemmas with honour and respect. If we are parents, we can learn how to teach our children the values of Bushido and how to raise them to be compassionate, responsible, and resilient. And if we are retirees, we can learn how to find new purpose and meaning in our lives and leave a legacy that reflects our deepest values.

The Everyday Samurai is a book that transcends age, culture, and background. It is a book that invites readers to reflect on their lives, values, and goals and take practical steps towards living a life of excellence. By embracing the principles of Bushido, readers can learn to live with purpose, meaning, and fulfilment and ultimately become the best versions of themselves.

The Everyday Samurai offers a ray of hope and guidance in a world that can often feel chaotic and uncertain. It reminds us that no matter what challenges we face, we can always choose to live with discipline, courage, and honour and that by doing so, we can positively impact the world around us. The Everyday Samurai is not just a book about the past; it is a book about the present and the future, and it has the power to inspire readers to become everyday samurai in their own lives.

The book is written for the intelligent, informed reader interested in personal growth, self-improvement, and living a life of meaning and purpose. The author assumes that the reader is familiar with basic concepts of psychology, philosophy, and self-help but does not assume any prior knowledge of Japanese history or culture. The book is accessible to anyone willing to learn and grow, regardless of their background or experience.

The author of The Everyday Samurai is a lifelong martial artist and a student of Japanese culture and philosophy. He is also a practising Lama in a school of Tibetan mystical Buddhism. He has spent years studying the principles of Bushido and how they can be applied to modern life. Through his research and personal experience, he has developed a deep understanding of the samurai way of life and how it can be adapted to contemporary society.

The author's goal in writing The Everyday Samurai is to provide readers with a practical and inspirational guide to living a life of purpose and fulfilment. He believes that the principles of Bushido offer a powerful framework for personal growth and self-improvement and that anyone can benefit from these teachings, regardless of their cultural background or personal beliefs.

In the book's first chapters, the author provides an overview of the history of the samurai and the code of Bushido. He explains how the samurai lived their lives, the values they held dear, and the challenges they faced. He also discusses the relevance of samurai culture to modern society and why the principles of Bushido are still important today. He looks at the origins of the bushido code and the religious and spiritual influences that created its unique character. He also examines the Samurai, their personalities, and stories, showing how they are remarkably similar to us, despite being separated by centuries.

Later in the book, eight chapters each focus on a specific principle of the samurai code, providing readers with practical tips and exercises to help them develop these traits in their own lives. For example, the chapter on respect offers advice on cultivating respect in your daily routine and looks at how we show respect for ourselves and those around us. At the same time, the chapter on self-control provides strategies for managing your emotions and impulses.

The author emphasises the importance of mindfulness, self-awareness, and introspection throughout the book. He encourages readers to reflect on their lives, values, and beliefs and consider how the Bushido principles can help them live more fulfilling and meaningful lives.

In the book's final chapter, the author summarises the key points and provides a final message of inspiration and motivation. He reminds readers that living a life of purpose and meaning is a journey that requires commitment, perseverance, and self-reflection. He encourages readers to continue practising the principles of Bushido in their daily lives and to strive for excellence in all they do.

The Everyday Samurai is more than just a self-help book. It's a roadmap for living a life of integrity, courage, and compassion. It's a call to action for anyone who wants to live their life with purpose and intention. By combining ancient wisdom with practical advice, the author has created a guide that is both inspirational and life-changing.

Whether you are looking to overcome personal challenges, achieve professional success, or simply live a more fulfilling life, The Everyday Samurai offers something for everyone. It's a book that will challenge, inspire, and motivate you to be the best version of yourself.

# SAMURAI CULTURE

**In many ways, the samurai were the embodiment of the warrior spirit, and their way of life offers a powerful example of what it means to live with integrity and courage. By studying samurai culture and the principles of Bushido, we can learn important lessons about leadership, personal growth, and the pursuit of excellence.**

The origins of samurai culture can be traced back to the early centuries of Japanese history. During the 8th century, the first Japanese warriors emerged, known as "bushi." The bushi were hired by local rulers to protect their lands and people from raiders, pirates, and other threats. The bushi were skilled in the art of warfare, and they were known for their bravery and fighting prowess.

As time went on, the bushi became more organised and began to develop a code of conduct that would come to be known as "bushido." This code of conduct emphasised virtues such as loyalty, courage, and self-discipline. The bushi believed that it was their duty to protect their lord and their community, even if it meant sacrificing their own lives in the process. They valued honour highly and believed it was better to die with honour than to live in shame.

The bushi also placed a great emphasis on physical fitness and martial training. They believed that a warrior must be physically strong and agile in order to be effective in combat. They trained extensively in swordsmanship, archery, and other martial arts and were known for their deadly accuracy and lightning-fast reflexes.

Over time, the bushi evolved into the samurai, a class of highly skilled warriors who would come to dominate Japanese society for centuries. The samurai continued to adhere to the principles of Bushido, and they developed their own unique culture and way of life. They were known for their strict discipline, unwavering loyalty, and unyielding courage.

In the 12th century, Japan was a fragmented land, divided into many small states, each with its own ruler. The constant power struggles between these rulers created a climate of instability and violence, and it was during this tumultuous period the samurai emerged as the dominant class. Initially, the samurai were hired by the rulers as their personal guards and administrators, but over time, they evolved into a powerful military caste that would play a significant role in Japanese history.

The samurai were renowned for their martial prowess, and they developed their own unique fighting style known as *kenjutsu*, which was based on the use of the sword. They also developed a highly disciplined and rigorous training system, emphasising physical fitness, mental focus, and spiritual development. Through this training, the samurai developed an unshakable confidence in their abilities and came to view themselves as invincible warriors.

As an example of the Samurai, let's look closely at one of the most famous samurai in Japanese history: Miyamoto Musashi. Musashi was a legendary swordsman who lived during the 17th century. He was renowned for his exceptional skills in swordsmanship and his undefeated record in over 60 duels.

Musashi was born into a samurai family but was orphaned at a young age and raised by his uncle, a Buddhist priest. Musashi began training in swordsmanship as a teenager, studying under various masters and engaging in duels to test his skills.

Musashi's style of swordsmanship, known as Niten Ichi-Ryu or "two swords as one," involved using both a long and short sword simultaneously. This technique allowed him to attack and defend simultaneously, giving him a significant advantage in battle.

Musashi's most famous duel was with Sasaki Kojiro, a skilled swordsman who was considered to be Musashi's greatest rival. The two men fought on a small island off the coast of Japan, with Musashi arriving late and using a wooden sword he had carved from an oar. Despite these disadvantages, Musashi defeated Kojiro in the duel and became legendary in Japanese history.

Musashi's legacy goes beyond his martial prowess. He also wrote "The Book of Five Rings," a famous treatise on strategy and martial arts. In this book, Musashi outlines his philosophy of swordsmanship, emphasising the importance of strategy, timing, and mental focus. His ideas have influenced not only martial arts but also business, politics, and other fields.

In addition to his accomplishments as a swordsman and philosopher, Musashi was also an accomplished artist and calligrapher. He created many famous works of art, including a series of ink paintings depicting his travels throughout Japan.

Miyamoto Musashi remains a beloved figure in Japanese culture, and his legacy continues to inspire people around the world. He embodied the values of samurai culture, including loyalty, honour, discipline, and courage, and his dedication to martial arts and philosophy continues to be celebrated to this day.

In addition to their martial prowess, the samurai were also known for their strict code of ethics, known as Bushido. This code emphasised virtues such as honour, courage, loyalty, and self-discipline, which became the samurai culture's guiding principle. The samurai believed that it was better to die with honour than to live in shame, and they placed a high value on personal integrity and self-control. Bushido was not just a set of rules to be followed but a way of life, permeating every aspect of samurai culture.

Bushido emphasised several fundamental values, including loyalty, honour, discipline, courage, and self-sacrifice. These values were deeply ingrained in the samurai way of life, influencing everything from how they dressed to how they fought.

One of the essential values in samurai culture was loyalty. Samurai were expected to be loyal to their lord above all else and willing to sacrifice their own lives for his sake. This loyalty was considered the foundation of the samurai way of life and was expected to be absolute and unwavering.

Honour was another strong value in samurai culture. Samurai were expected to live with integrity and honour and always uphold their reputation. Dishonourable behaviour was considered a grave offence, and samurai who were found to be dishonourable could be punished severely.

Discipline was also a key value in samurai culture. Samurai were expected to live with strict self-discipline and always adhere to a strict code of conduct. This discipline extended to every aspect of their lives, from their daily routines to their behaviour on the battlefield.

Courage was another critical value in samurai culture. Samurai were expected to be fearless in battle and willing to face death without hesitation. This courage was not just physical but also moral and spiritual, and it was considered an essential aspect of the samurai's way of life.

Self-sacrifice was also a fundamental value in samurai culture. Samurai were expected to be willing to sacrifice their own lives for the greater good, whether that meant defending their lord, their family, or their country. This self-sacrifice was considered the ultimate expression of loyalty and honour and was highly valued in samurai culture.

Samurai culture also emphasised the importance of education and the pursuit of knowledge. Samurai were expected to be well-educated and knowledgeable about a wide range of subjects, including poetry, art, philosophy, and politics. This education was essential for developing a well-rounded individual who could serve his lord and country with wisdom and intelligence.

The samurai were also known for their martial arts skills, which they developed through rigorous training and discipline. These skills included sword fighting, archery, horseback riding, and hand-to-hand combat. Samurai were expected to be highly skilled in these arts, as they were essential for protecting their lord and their country.

Another critical aspect of samurai culture was aesthetics. Samurai were known for their appreciation of beauty and their love of nature. They were skilled in the arts of calligraphy, flower arrangement, and tea ceremony, and they often incorporated these activities into their daily routines. The samurai believed these activities helped cultivate a sense of inner peace and harmony, and they viewed them as essential aspects of their overall training.

Samurai culture evolved and changed throughout the centuries, reflecting Japan's political and social changes. However, the core values of Bushido remained constant, and they continued to influence Japanese culture long after the samurai themselves had disappeared.

Today, samurai culture continues to inspire people around the world. The values of loyalty, honour, discipline, courage, and self-sacrifice are timeless and offer important lessons for anyone who wishes to live a life of purpose and meaning. In many ways, the samurai were the embodiment of the warrior spirit, and their way of life offers a powerful example of what it means to live with integrity and courage. By studying samurai culture and the principles of Bushido, we can learn important lessons about leadership, personal growth, and the pursuit of excellence.

The samurai were known for their unwavering loyalty to their lord, steadfast dedication to their craft, and willingness to face any challenge with courage and grace. These values are just as relevant today as they were centuries ago. In a world where we are often pulled in different directions and faced with conflicting priorities, losing sight of what is truly important can be easy. The samurai remind us that our loyalty to our values and commitment to personal excellence is essential to living a life of purpose and meaning.

Whether we are leaders in our communities or simply seeking to live our lives with purpose and intention, samurai culture's wisdom can help us achieve our goals and become the best version of ourselves. It offers a roadmap for living a life of honour, courage, and self-discipline, and it reminds us of the importance of being true to ourselves and our values, even in the face of adversity. By cultivating the inner strength and resilience needed to face life's challenges with grace and courage, we can become the kind of leaders and individuals who make a positive difference in the world.

# THE SWORD

---

**The katana stands as a powerful metaphor for the samurai's spirituality, reminding us of the importance of living a life guided by honour, discipline, and selflessness. Its legacy continues to inspire us to this day, a testament to the enduring power of the samurai's spirit and their unwavering dedication to living a life of meaning and purpose.**

---

The katana, the iconic sword of the samurai, is not just a weapon but a work of art. The process of crafting a katana was a meticulous and time-consuming one, requiring both technical expertise and artistic vision. The process of creating a katana involved many stages, each requiring careful attention to detail.

The first step in creating a katana was to select suitable materials. The blade was made from *tamahagane*, a type of steel produced by smelting iron sand with charcoal in a *tatara* furnace. This process required many hours of work, as the tamahagane needed to be heated, hammered, and folded over and over again until it reached the desired consistency.

Once the *tamahagane* had been prepared, it was time to begin forging the blade. This was done using a technique called *tanren*, which involved repeatedly heating and hammering the metal until it took on the desired shape and thickness. This process could take days or even weeks, depending on the smith's skill and the blade's size.

But the forging process was not just about creating a strong, durable blade. It was also about imbuing the sword with spiritual energy, or *ki*. The smiths believed that the sword was an extension of the samurai's spirit and that the blade's quality reflected the samurai's character.

As such, the forging process was as much a test of the smith's character as it was a test of his technical skill. It required patience, discipline, and a willingness to endure long hours of hard work in order to achieve perfection.

In this way, the process of crafting a katana became a metaphor for the forging of the human spirit. Just as the sword was tempered and strengthened through the process of tanren, so too could the samurai strengthen his character and hone his spirit through the challenges of life.

The final result of this painstaking process was a deadly weapon and a work of art. The unique pattern on the blade, known as the *hamon*, was created by the differential hardening process, in which the blade was heated and cooled at different rates. The result was a beautiful and intricate pattern unique to each blade.

The beauty and artistry of the katana were not lost on the samurai. They saw the sword as not only a tool for war but also a symbol of their status and identity as warriors. The samurai would often give their swords names, and they would be passed down from generation to generation as family heirlooms.

In addition to its physical power, the katana was also considered a metaphor for truth and cutting through delusions and lies. The samurai believed the sword represented the truth and could cut through any falsehood or illusion. The samurai were trained to see beyond appearances and to focus on the essence of things. The sword was a tool for cutting through the world's distractions and staying focused on what truly mattered.

The sword metaphor can also be applied to our modern lives. In a world filled with distractions and misinformation, staying focused on what truly matters can be challenging. The samurai believed that the key to success was to remain focused and cut through the world's distractions. We can apply this same philosophy to our own lives by staying focused on our goals and cutting through the distractions that get in the way.

Another way in which the metaphor of the sword can be applied to modern life is through the concept of discipline. The samurai were renowned for their discipline and dedication to their craft. They spent years perfecting their skills and honing their abilities. Similarly, we can apply this same discipline and dedication to our own lives by developing our skills and working towards our goals with persistence and determination.

The samurai sword also represents the concept of mindfulness. The samurai believed that the sword was an extension of their minds and that they needed to be fully present and aware when using it. They were trained to be mindful of their surroundings, opponents, thoughts and emotions. This mindfulness helped them stay focused and make quick decisions in battle.

We can apply this same concept of mindfulness to our lives by being fully present and aware of our surroundings, thoughts, and emotions. By developing our mindfulness, we can stay focused and make better decisions in our personal and professional lives.

In modern times, the katana has become a symbol of Japanese culture and is admired by people all over the world. But the lessons that can be learned from the process of crafting a katana are still relevant today. The idea of tanren, of forging oneself through hard work and perseverance, is just as applicable to modern life as it was to the samurai.

The samurai sword is a powerful symbol of the samurai's discipline, honour, and mental fortitude. As a metaphor for truth and mindfulness, it teaches us to stay focused on our goals, develop our skills, and be aware of our surroundings and emotions. The katana, in particular, embodies the samurai spirit and serves as a reminder that true strength comes from a strong mind and spirit, not just physical prowess.

The process of crafting a katana is a testament to the samurai's discipline, patience, and endurance. It is not just a weapon but a work of art showcasing the swordsmith's technical skill and artistry. The forging of a katana serves as a reminder to us all to strive for excellence and to endure hardship in order to forge ourselves into stronger individuals. The lessons learned from forging a katana are as relevant today as they were in samurai times, inspiring us to pursue personal growth and excellence in all aspects of our lives.

In modern times, the sword's equivalents can be found in pursuing personal growth, excellence, and discipline. These pursuits require a strong mind, a resilient spirit, and an unwavering dedication to one's goals. Like the swordsmiths who crafted the katana, modern individuals must endure challenges, setbacks, and failures to emerge stronger, more capable, and more focused on what truly matters.

The sword's metaphorical and spiritual meanings can also be applied to various aspects of modern life. For instance, mindfulness, central to the samurai's use of the sword, can be applied to multiple fields, such as sports, business, and mental health. The ability to be fully present, aware, and focused is crucial in achieving success and satisfaction in these fields.

Similarly, the idea of cutting through distractions and focusing on what truly matters is relevant to modern life. In a world full of distractions, misinformation, and noise, staying focused on one's goals and values is essential for personal growth and success. The sword can serve as a reminder to cut through the noise and to stay true to one's principles.

So, we see the sword is not just a weapon but a symbol of culture, identity, and personal growth. Its metaphorical and spiritual meanings still apply in modern times, inspiring individuals to pursue excellence, discipline, and mindfulness in their personal and professional lives. The sword's legacy is a testament to the human spirit's ability to endure challenges, overcome obstacles, and forge itself into something stronger and more resilient.

"The katana's sleek and elegant design embodies the samurai's commitment to simplicity, discipline, and the pursuit of perfection. The long, slender sword represents the samurai's unrelenting focus, cutting through all obstacles in their path with swift and decisive action.

But the true significance of the katana lies not in its physical attributes but in the mindset it represents. For the samurai, the sword was not just a tool for combat but a reflection of their innermost being. It embodied their code of Bushido, a way of life that emphasised loyalty, courage, and self-sacrifice"

# WABI-SABI KINTSUGI

Wabi-sabi and kintsugi embody the essence of samurai thinking, valuing simplicity, imperfection, and the beauty of ageing and decay. The art of repairing broken objects with gold mirrors the samurai's emphasis on honour, resilience, and turning adversity into strength.

The concepts of wabi-sabi and kintsugi are deeply ingrained in Japanese culture and have significant relevance to the samurai way of life. Wabi-sabi refers to a worldview centred on the acceptance of impermanence and imperfection, while kintsugi is the art of repairing broken pottery with gold lacquer. Together, they represent a powerful metaphor for the samurai's approach to life and their philosophy of resilience.

*"Wabi-sabi is the beauty of things imperfect, impermanent, and incomplete. It is the beauty of things modest and humble. It is the beauty of things unconventional."* - Leonard Koren. Wabi-Sabi for Artists, Designers, Poets & Philosophers

In samurai culture, wabi-sabi was a way of life. It was an understanding that nothing in life is perfect and everything is in a state of constant change. Samurai were trained to embrace life's impermanence and find beauty in the imperfect and the transitory. This philosophy was reflected in many aspects of samurai life, including their appreciation for the beauty of nature, their love of simple and austere aesthetics, and their acceptance of death as an inevitable part of life.

*"Not only is there no need to hide flaws, but the imperfections are precisely what make things memorable and valuable."* - Donald Richie. The Japanese Sense of Beauty

Kintsugi, on the other hand, was a practical application of wabi-sabi. It was a way of repairing broken pottery that restored the object to its former beauty and elevated it to a higher level of aesthetic value. The gold lacquer used to repair the broken pieces created a visual reminder of the object's history and its struggles. The result was a new object that was not only beautiful but also unique and imbued with a deeper meaning.

The practice of kintsugi had a profound philosophical significance for the samurai. It represented their belief that adversity and challenge were essential components of life and that the scars and imperfections resulting from those challenges were not things to be hidden or ashamed of but celebrated and valued. It was a way of embracing the reality of life and finding beauty and meaning in even the most difficult and trying times.

*"The art of kintsugi teaches that brokenness can be transformed into something beautiful and unique. What a powerful metaphor for the human experience."* - Minaa B. Rivers Are Coming: Essays and Poems on Healing

Today, the concepts of wabi-sabi and kintsugi remain relevant in modern society. In a world that often values perfection and flawlessness, wabi-sabi offers a liberating perspective. It reminds us that imperfection is not only natural but can also be beautiful and meaningful. It encourages us to embrace our imperfections and scars and find beauty and strength in our challenges and struggles.

*"The beauty of wabi-sabi lies in its simplicity, its imperfection, and its authenticity. It reminds us that true beauty is not found in perfection but in the natural, the unadorned, and the honest."* - Robyn Griggs Lawrence. The Wabi-Sabi House: The Japanese Art of Imperfect Beauty

Similarly, kintsugi teaches us that even brokenness can be transformed into something beautiful and valuable. It reminds us that the scars and imperfections we carry with us are not things to be hidden or ashamed of but rather sources of strength and resilience. We can create something new and beautiful that reflects our unique journeys by repairing the broken pieces of our lives with the "gold lacquer" of our experiences and wisdom.

In conclusion, the concepts of wabi-sabi and kintsugi have profound relevance to the samurai way of life and offer valuable lessons for us today. They remind us that imperfection and brokenness are not things to be feared or avoided but instead embraced and celebrated. By embracing the impermanence and imperfection of life and finding beauty and meaning in even the most challenging times, we can live a life of strength, resilience, and beauty.

権兵衛
権兵衛
祇園いづ重
祇園いづ重
祇園いづ重
茂山童司
舞扇堂
舞扇堂
次朗
矢野一郎
矢野一郎
矢野一郎
水口弥
安藤孝子
凜香
池田家
小愛
小松陽一郎
伊原友己
八坂神社

# RELIGION AND SPIRITUALITY IN SAMURAI LIFE

Spirituality played a vital role in shaping samurai culture, influencing both their code of Bushido and way of life. Rooted in Zen Buddhism and Shintoism, their spiritual beliefs emphasised discipline, humility, and detachment from worldly desires. By cultivating inner strength and wisdom through their spiritual practice, the samurai aimed to achieve mastery in all areas of life, including combat, art, and governance.

The samurai are often portrayed as fierce warriors who were primarily concerned with martial prowess and combat skills. However, the reality is far more nuanced than this simplistic portrayal. The samurai were, in fact, educated and cultivated men who valued spiritual and intellectual pursuits as much as they loved martial ones. They were seekers of wisdom and knowledge, always striving to improve themselves and better understand the world around them.

Religion played a crucial role in the lives of the samurai, providing them with guidance and inspiration as they navigated the challenges of their existence. Over the centuries, various religious traditions influenced samurai culture, profoundly shaping their beliefs, attitudes, and practices.

In this chapter, we will explore the influence and importance of religions in samurai culture, examining the ways in which various faiths contributed to the development of this unique way of life. We will delve into the teachings of Zen Buddhism, which became a dominant force in samurai culture during the Kamakura period. We will also look at Confucianism, which emphasised the importance of duty, loyalty, and social order and was adopted by many samurai as a guiding philosophy.

In addition, we will examine the role of Shintoism, the indigenous religion of Japan, in shaping samurai culture and explore the ways in which Christianity, Taoism, and Hinduism influenced the samurai worldview. We will discuss how the samurai were open to new ideas and spiritual influences, always seeking to expand their understanding of the world and their place within it.

We will also examine how the samurai's proximity to death influenced their spiritual outlook, causing them to focus on the importance of living in the present moment and cultivating a deep sense of inner peace and balance. We will see how the samurai's education and training helped them develop the mental and spiritual fortitude necessary to face the challenges of their existence with courage and equanimity.

In the end, we will come to see that the samurai were not just warriors but also spiritual seekers, drawing inspiration from a range of religious traditions to create a unique way of life that emphasised the importance of discipline, honour, and self-control. The legacy of the samurai lives on to this day, reminding us of the power of spiritual cultivation and the importance of living with integrity and purpose.

## THE IMPORTANCE OF ZEN IN SAMURAI CULTURE

Zen Buddhism significantly shaped samurai culture in Japan, influencing their way of life, ethical codes, and martial arts. Zen philosophy emphasised the practice of meditation and mindfulness, which became integral to the samurai's approach to life and combat. In this section, we will explore the importance and influence of Zen in samurai culture, highlighting its use with examples from samurai history and literature.

Zen Buddhism, which originated in China and spread to Japan in the 12th century, was primarily concerned with the attainment of enlightenment through meditation and the practice of mindfulness. It emphasised the present moment, letting go of attachments, and the realisation of the true nature of reality. Zen Buddhism became popular among samurai, who were drawn to its teachings on discipline, mental focus, and the cultivation of inner strength.

*"In the beginner's mind, there are many possibilities, but in the expert's mind, there are few."* - Shunryu Suzuki, Zen master

One of the most significant ways that Zen influenced samurai culture was through the development of Zen Buddhism as a martial art. Zen masters recognised the potential for the practice of Zen to enhance the physical abilities of samurai warriors, and they began to incorporate martial arts training into their teachings. Zen archery, swordsmanship, and hand-to-hand combat became popular among samurai practitioners, emphasising the importance of mental focus, breath control, and mindfulness in martial arts.

The Zen-inspired martial arts helped develop the samurai's physical abilities and combat skills, reinforcing their ethical codes and values. Zen emphasised the importance of self-discipline, humility, and respect for others, values that were already integral to the samurai's code of Bushido. The samurai warriors saw themselves as both protectors of their lord and defenders of the social order, and the practice of Zen helped to reinforce their sense of duty and honour.

*"The ultimate aim of the art of karate lies not in victory or defeat, but in the perfection of the character of its participants."* - Gichin Funakoshi, founder of Shotokan karate

One of the most famous examples of the influence of Zen in samurai culture can be seen in the life and teachings of Miyamoto Musashi. Musashi was a legendary swordsman who lived in the 17th century and is considered one of the greatest samurai in Japanese history. Musashi was a skilled warrior and a Zen practitioner who incorporated Zen philosophy into his martial arts training.

Musashi's teachings emphasised the importance of mental focus, simplicity, and the cultivation of inner strength. He believed that the ultimate goal of the samurai was not victory in battle but the realisation of the true nature of reality. Musashi's book, "The Book of Five Rings," which outlines his martial arts philosophy, became a classic text of samurai culture and is still studied by martial artists and Zen practitioners today.

*"The art of swordsmanship is the art of controlling the mind."* - Yamaoka Tesshu, 19th-century samurai and Zen master

Another example of the influence of Zen in samurai culture can be seen in the practice of Zen meditation. Zen meditation, or zazen, was a crucial part of Zen philosophy, and samurai warriors widely practised it. Zazen helped to cultivate mental focus, discipline, and the ability to remain calm and centred under pressure, qualities that were essential to the samurai's way of life.

*"The mind is everything. What you think, you become."* - Buddha

The influence of Zen in samurai culture can also be seen in Japanese art and design aesthetics. Zen-inspired art, such as calligraphy and ink paintings, emphasised simplicity, elegance, and the beauty of imperfection.

*"Beauty is in imperfection."* - Japanese proverb

These values were also reflected in the design of samurai swords, prized for their sharpness, durability, beauty, and craftsmanship.

Zen Buddhism significantly impacted samurai culture in Japan, influencing various aspects of their way of life, including ethical codes, martial arts, and daily practices. Zen philosophy emphasised meditation and mindfulness, which became integral to the samurai's approach to life and combat. Zen-inspired martial arts helped develop the samurai's physical abilities and combat skills while reinforcing their ethical codes and values. The teachings of Zen masters, particularly Miyamoto Musashi, are still studied and admired today as a classic text of samurai culture.

Zen meditation also helped cultivate mental focus, discipline, and the ability to remain calm and centred under pressure - qualities essential to the samurai's way of life.

Moreover, Zen aesthetics, emphasising simplicity, elegance, and beauty, influenced samurai culture and Japanese art and design.

Today, the influence of Zen on samurai culture can still be observed through the continued study and practice of Zen-inspired martial arts, such as aikido and kendo, which prioritise mental focus, breath control, and mindfulness. Miyamoto Musashi's teachings and other Zen masters' philosophies continue to inspire martial artists and practitioners of Zen today.

Undoubtedly, Zen philosophy has become an integral part of Japanese culture, with its teachings on mindfulness and present-moment awareness influencing many aspects of modern-day Japanese life. The practice of Zen meditation remains popular in Japan, with many people attending Zen retreats and centres to cultivate mental focus and inner peace.

In conclusion, the impact of Zen on samurai culture is undeniable. Zen philosophy was crucial in shaping the samurai's approach to life and combat. Zen-inspired martial arts reinforced their ethical codes and values while developing their physical abilities and combat skills. Today, the teachings of Zen masters continue to inspire martial artists and practitioners of Zen, and the influence of Zen can still be seen in modern-day Japan's emphasis on mindfulness and present-moment awareness

## THE IMPORTANCE OF CONFUCIANISM IN SAMURAI CULTURE

Confucianism is another major philosophical and ethical tradition that profoundly impacted samurai culture. Confucian teachings emphasised the importance of social order, morality, and duty and provided a framework for ethical behaviour and personal conduct. For the samurai, Confucianism offered a set of ethical principles that complemented their martial training and helped to shape their approach to life and society.

One of Confucianism's central tenets was filial piety, which emphasised the importance of respect and obedience to one's parents and ancestors. This concept was particularly relevant to the samurai, who strongly emphasised loyalty, obedience, and respect for authority. Samurai were expected to be obedient to their lords and superiors and to place the needs of their clan and country above their own individual interests. The concept of filial piety also extended to the samurai's duty to protect their family and clan, even at the cost of their own lives.

Another important Confucian principle that influenced samurai culture was the concept of the "gentleman," or "Junzi," which emphasised the importance of moral virtue, wisdom, and personal conduct. The concept of the Junzi encouraged the samurai to cultivate virtues such as honesty, courage, and compassion and to avoid vices such as arrogance, greed, and cruelty. The concept of the Junzi also helped to reinforce the samurai's role as ethical leaders in society. It encouraged them to use their martial skills to protect and serve their community.

The concept of loyalty was also central to Confucianism and samurai culture. Confucian teachings emphasised the importance of loyalty to one's family, clan, and country, and the samurai were expected to be unwaveringly loyal to their lords and superiors. Loyalty was considered one of the highest virtues of the samurai, and many samurai were willing to die for their lords and clans in times of war or crisis. This concept of loyalty also extended to the samurai's duty to protect the weak and vulnerable in society and uphold justice and righteousness in their dealings with others.

One of the most famous samurai who embodied Confucian ideals was the legendary warrior Takeda Shingen. Takeda was known for his strict adherence to Confucian principles and was renowned for his wisdom, courage, and moral integrity. He was also a master strategist and tactician and was able to use his military skills to protect his clan and expand his influence in feudal Japan. Takeda's legacy as a model samurai leader is still celebrated in Japan today, and he remains an inspiration to many martial artists and students of Confucian philosophy.

The influence of Confucianism on samurai culture can also be seen in the development of Bushido, or the "way of the warrior." Bushido was a code of ethics that emerged during the Edo period in Japan and was heavily influenced by Confucian teachings. Bushido emphasised the importance of loyalty, filial piety, courage, and other virtues that were central to Confucian philosophy. The bushido code also provided a framework for the samurai's martial training and helped shape their approach to combat and warfare.

In conclusion, Confucianism significantly impacted samurai culture, providing a set of ethical principles that complemented their martial training and helped shape their approach to life and society. The emphasis on filial piety, loyalty, and moral virtue provided a framework for the samurai's ethical behaviour and personal conduct. At the same time, the concept of the Junzi reinforced their role as ethical leaders in society. The influence of Confucianism on samurai culture can still be seen in modern-day Japan, where the legacy of the samurai continues to be celebrated and studied. The enduring influence of Confucianism on samurai culture is a testament to the enduring relevance of these ethical principles, which continue to inspire people around the world to live lives of wisdom, courage, and moral integrity.

## THE IMPORTANCE OF SHINTOISM IN SAMURAI CULTURE

Shintoism is a religion that has significantly influenced the culture and worldview of the samurai. As the indigenous religion of Japan, it is deeply rooted in the country's history, mythology, and cultural identity. Shintoism emphasises the veneration of ancestors and spirits and holds that every aspect of the natural world is imbued with a divine presence. This belief system helped shape the samurai's ethical and spiritual outlook and contributed to their sense of duty, honour, and loyalty.

One of the key aspects of Shintoism that influenced samurai culture was its emphasis on purity and cleanliness. Shinto teachings held that purity was essential for spiritual and physical well-being and that impurity could bring misfortune and illness. As a result, the samurai adopted many Shinto purification rituals, such as washing their hands and faces before battle and performing elaborate purification ceremonies at Shinto shrines.

Shintoism also played a role in shaping the samurai's sense of duty and loyalty. The religion emphasises the importance of one's ancestors and heritage and holds that individuals have a responsibility to honour and uphold the legacy of their forebears. This concept of filial piety was central to samurai culture and formed the basis of their code of ethics and conduct. The samurai believed that it was their duty to serve their lords and masters with loyalty and devotion and to uphold the honour of their families and clans.

Shintoism also profoundly influenced the art and aesthetics of the samurai. The religion held that everything in the natural world was imbued with a divine spirit and that the beauty of nature was a reflection of this spiritual essence. As a result, the samurai developed a deep appreciation for the natural world and sought to incorporate its beauty into their artistic and cultural practices. This is evident in the intricate designs of their armour and weaponry, which often feature motifs inspired by nature, such as animals, flowers, and landscapes.

Shintoism also played a role in the ritualised aspects of samurai culture. Shinto shrines were often built on the grounds of samurai castles and were used as a focal points for various rituals and ceremonies. The samurai would visit these shrines before battle to offer prayers for victory and perform purification rituals before important events such as weddings and funerals. Shintoism's rituals and ceremonies helped reinforce the samurai's sense of community and identity. They served as a reminder of their duty to uphold the honour and legacy of their ancestors.

One of the most famous examples of the influence of Shintoism on samurai culture is the story of the 47 Ronin. In 1701, Lord Asano Naganori was ordered to entertain the imperial envoy Kira Yoshinaka but became enraged when Kira insulted him. As a result, Asano drew his sword and attacked Kira, for which he was ordered to commit seppuku (ritual suicide). His retainers were left without a lord and disgraced in society's eyes. However, instead of seeking revenge or surrendering to their fate, the samurai decided to honour their lord's memory by seeking vengeance on Kira. After a year of planning and preparation, they stormed Kira's mansion and killed him before surrendering themselves to the authorities. The 47 Ronin were then ordered to commit seppuku. However, their act of loyalty and devotion to their lord became legendary in Japanese history and is still celebrated as an example of the samurai code of honour and loyalty.

In conclusion, Shintoism was a powerful influence on samurai culture, shaping their sense of duty, honour, and loyalty, as well as their appreciation for the natural world and the ritualised aspects of their society. Shinto teachings helped shape the samurai's ethical and spiritual outlook and contributed to their deep sense of obligation to their lord, family, and community. The religion's emphasis on purity and cleanliness also played a role in the samurai's daily routines, with many purification rituals becoming an integral part of their martial practices.

The aesthetic and artistic sensibilities of Shintoism also had a profound impact on samurai culture. The belief that everything in nature was imbued with a divine spirit led to a reverence for nature and a deep appreciation for its beauty. This reverence for nature was reflected in the intricate designs of their armour and weaponry, which often incorporated natural motifs such as animals, flowers, and landscapes. Additionally, the importance of ritual and ceremony in Shintoism was reflected in the elaborate rituals and ceremonies that accompanied many aspects of samurai life, including weddings, funerals, and battles.

Shintoism played a significant role in shaping the culture and worldview of the samurai. Its emphasis on duty, loyalty, and honour contributed to the development of the samurai code, while its teachings on purity and cleanliness influenced their daily routines and martial practices. Additionally, the religion's emphasis on the natural world and its beauty influenced the artistic and aesthetic sensibilities of the samurai, leading to the creation of some of the most iconic and beautiful works of art and weaponry in Japanese history.

## THE INFLUENCE OF CHRISTIANITY ON SAMURAI CULTURE

The influence of Christianity on samurai culture is a relatively lesser-known aspect of their history. Still, it nonetheless played an important role in shaping the worldview and beliefs of some samurai during the late feudal period. The arrival of Christian missionaries in Japan in the 16th century marked the beginning of a complex relationship between the samurai and Christianity, with some embracing the religion. In contrast, others saw it as threatening traditional Japanese values and customs.

The Jesuit missionaries who arrived in Japan in the mid-16th century were initially welcomed by the ruling class, including some samurai, who saw their presence as an opportunity to gain access to European technology and knowledge. Many samurai were fascinated by the teachings of Christianity, which emphasised the importance of love, forgiveness, and humility, and were drawn to the religion's message of universal brotherhood.

One of the most notable examples of a samurai who converted to Christianity was Omura Sumitada, a daimyo who ruled over Nagasaki province in the late 16th century. Sumitada was introduced to Christianity by the Jesuit missionary Francis Xavier and eventually became a fervent convert, even going so far as to build a church in Nagasaki and establish a seminary to train Japanese priests. However, Sumitada's embrace of Christianity was not without controversy, and many of his retainers and other samurai saw it as a betrayal of traditional Japanese values.

Despite these challenges, Christianity continued to spread among the samurai during the Edo period, with many drawn to its message of equality and social justice. The religion's emphasis on charity and service to others also appealed to many samurai, who saw it as a way to fulfil their duty to society and to atone for the violence and bloodshed of their profession.

One of the most notable Christian samurai of the Edo period was Takayama Ukon, a daimyo who converted to Christianity in the late 16th century and remained a devout believer for the rest of his life. Takayama was known for his piety and devotion to the Church and was eventually exiled from Japan for refusing to renounce his faith. Despite this, his example inspired many other samurai to embrace Christianity, and his legacy continues to be celebrated in Japan today.

However, as Christianity continued to spread in Japan, it began to come into conflict with the Tokugawa shogunate, which saw it as a threat to the stability and unity of Japanese society. In 1614, the shogunate issued an edict banning Christianity and ordering all Christian missionaries to leave the country. This marked the beginning of a brutal period of persecution for Japanese Christians, including many samurai who had converted to the faith.

Despite this persecution, Christianity continued to survive in Japan and even played a role in the Meiji Restoration of the 19th century. Many of the leaders of the

Restoration were Christian converts, including Takayama Ukon's descendant, Ōkubo Toshimichi, who helped to establish the modern Japanese state.

In conclusion, Christianity played a complex and controversial role in samurai culture, with some embracing it as a path to personal redemption and social justice. In contrast, others saw it as threatening traditional Japanese values and customs. Nonetheless, its influence can still be felt in Japan today, and the legacy of Christian samurai such as Takayama Ukon continues to inspire and challenge us to this day

## THE INFLUENCE OF TAOISM ON SAMURAI CULTURE

Taoism, a philosophy and religious tradition originating in ancient China, has also influenced samurai culture throughout Japanese history. The principles of Taoism emphasise the importance of living in harmony with nature, cultivating a sense of inner peace, and embracing the natural flow of life. These concepts align with the samurai ideals of discipline, honour, and self-control, and as a result, Taoism has been an important influence on the development of the samurai ethos.

One of the critical elements of Taoism that resonated with the samurai was the idea of *wu-wei*, or "non-action." This concept refers to the notion that sometimes the best course of action is to do nothing and that one should allow events to unfold naturally without trying to control or manipulate them. This idea is reflected in the samurai concept of mushin, or "no mind," which refers to the state of mind that allows one to act spontaneously and without hesitation in the face of danger.

Another essential aspect of Taoism that influenced the samurai was the concept of yin and yang, which represents the balance between opposing forces in the universe. This concept was reflected in the samurai ideal of harmony, which emphasised the importance of balancing one's physical and spiritual well-being and balancing one's duty to society with one's personal aspirations.

Taoist concepts also found their way into the practice of martial arts, which were an essential part of the samurai way of life. The principles of Taoism, such as the importance of fluidity, spontaneity, and harmony, were reflected in the movements and techniques of many martial arts styles, including swordsmanship, archery, and hand-to-hand combat.

One of the most prominent samurai figures influenced by Taoism was Miyamoto Musashi, a renowned swordsman and philosopher who lived during the 17th century. Musashi was known for his innovative sword techniques and philosophical writings, reflecting his deep understanding of Taoist and Zen principles. His most famous work, The Book of Five Rings, is considered a classic text on martial arts strategy and has been studied by martial artists and businesspeople alike.

Musashi's philosophy emphasised the importance of adapting to changing circumstances and using natural instincts and intuition to guide actions. This idea is reflected in the Taoist concept of "going with the flow," which emphasises the importance of embracing change and allowing events to unfold naturally.

Another samurai figure who Taoism influenced was Yagyū Munenori, a prominent swordsman and advisor to the Tokugawa shogunate in the early 17th century. Munenori's philosophy emphasised the importance of developing one's inner strength and discipline. He believed that the key to success in life was to cultivate a sense of inner peace and harmony. His writings on the art of the sword, known as The Life-Giving Sword, reflected his deep understanding of Taoist and Zen principles.

In conclusion, Taoism has shaped the samurai ethos throughout Japanese history. Its emphasis on living in harmony with nature, embracing change, and developing inner peace and discipline aligns with the ideals of the samurai, and its influence can be seen in the philosophy and techniques of martial arts as well as in the writings of prominent samurai figures such as Miyamoto Musashi and Yagyū Munenori. The legacy of Taoism continues to inspire and challenge us to this day. Its principles remain relevant to anyone seeking to cultivate a sense of inner peace and balance in their lives.

## THE INFLUENCE OF HINDUISM IN SAMURAI CULTURE

Hinduism, a religion that originated in ancient India, has had some influence on samurai culture throughout Japanese history. This influence can be traced back to the spread of Buddhism from India to China and Japan. As Buddhism spread throughout Japan, it was often blended with local religious traditions, including Shintoism and Taoism, creating a unique blend of spiritual beliefs and practices that influenced the samurai way of life.

One of the key concepts from Hinduism that found its way into samurai culture was the idea of karma or the law of cause and effect. This concept suggests that one's actions have consequences, and one's current circumstances result from past actions. This idea is reflected in the samurai concept of Bushido, which emphasises the importance of living with honour and integrity and the belief that one's actions directly impact one's fate.

Another concept from Hinduism that influenced samurai culture was the idea of dharma, or one's duty or role in life. In Hinduism, one's dharma is determined by one's caste or social status, and it is believed that fulfilling one's duty is essential to achieving spiritual liberation. This idea resonated with the samurai, who saw themselves as warriors with a duty to protect their lords and uphold the social order.

The Hindu concept of moksha, or liberation from the cycle of birth and death, also found its way into samurai culture. This concept emphasises the importance of achieving spiritual enlightenment and transcending the limitations of the material world. While the samurai did not necessarily believe in reincarnation, they did believe in the importance of transcending one's limitations and achieving a higher level of consciousness.

One of the most famous samurai figures influenced by Hinduism was the warrior monk Sōhei Saigō, who lived during the 16th century. Saigō was known for his fierce fighting skills and commitment to Buddhism, which he blended with elements of Hinduism and Shintoism. He believed that martial arts and spiritual practice were inseparable and that both aimed to achieve enlightenment and transcendence.

Saigō's teachings emphasised the importance of meditation and spiritual practice and the need to cultivate a sense of inner peace and balance. His teachings were influential in developing the samurai ethos, and his legacy can be seen in the writings and teachings of other prominent samurai figures, such as Miyamoto Musashi and Yagyū Munenori.

Another samurai figure Hinduism influenced was Takeda Shingen, a powerful warlord who lived during the 16th century. Shingen was known for his strategic brilliance on the battlefield and his deep understanding of spiritual principles. His teachings blended elements of Buddhism, Hinduism, and Shintoism, emphasising the importance of balance, discipline, and self-control.

Shingen's teachings were influential in developing the samurai ethos. His legacy can be seen in the writings and teachings of other prominent samurai figures, such as the legendary swordsman and philosopher Miyamoto Musashi. Musashi was known for his innovative techniques and his deep understanding of martial arts strategy, and Hindu and Buddhist principles heavily influenced his philosophy.

In conclusion, Hinduism has had some influence on samurai culture throughout Japanese history, mainly through the spread of Buddhism from India to Japan. The concepts of karma, dharma, and moksha found their way into the samurai ethos. The teachings of prominent samurai figures such as Sōhei Saigō and Takeda Shingen reflected these influences. The legacy of Hinduism continues to inspire and challenge us to this day. Its principles remain relevant to anyone seeking to achieve spiritual enlightenment and transcend beyond the limitations of the material world. While Hinduism did not originate in Japan, its influence on samurai culture demonstrates the universal appeal of its principles, emphasising the importance of living a virtuous and disciplined life, pursuing knowledge and wisdom, and striving for inner peace and harmony. These ideas are as relevant today as they were centuries ago and continue to inspire people from all walks of life to seek spiritual growth and transformation. The samurai, in particular, serve as a powerful example of how these principles can be put into practice in a way that emphasises the importance of honour, duty, and service to others. Their legacy lives on as a testament to the enduring influence of Hinduism on Japanese culture and society and as a source of inspiration for anyone seeking to live a life of purpose and meaning.

Throughout Japanese history, the samurai were known not only as fierce warriors but also as spiritual seekers who were open to new ideas and influences from a variety of religious traditions. Their education was focused not only on the art of war but also on literature, philosophy, and spiritual practices, reflecting their belief in the importance of cultivating the mind, spirit, and body.

The samurai lived in a world where death was a constant presence, and this proximity to mortality profoundly impacted their worldview. They understood that life was fleeting and that every moment was precious. This awareness of the impermanence of life led them to value spiritual knowledge and seek out wisdom from various sources.

The samurai were not tied to any particular religious tradition but were open to learning from various sources. They were influenced by Buddhism, Confucianism, Taoism, Shintoism, and even Hinduism, as we have seen in the previous section. The samurai believed that there was wisdom to be gained from each of these traditions and that by integrating these diverse perspectives into their own worldview, they could better understand the world and their place in it.

The samurai were highly disciplined and dedicated to their craft, and this discipline extended to their spiritual practices as well. They believed true martial arts mastery could only be achieved by cultivating inner peace, balance, and control. This required a deep understanding of spiritual principles and a commitment to ongoing spiritual practice.

The samurai were not just warriors but also poets, philosophers, and spiritual seekers. They understood that true strength came not just from physical prowess but also from mental and spiritual fortitude. This understanding led them to value discipline, honour, and self-control above all else and live purposefully and meaningfully.

Ultimately, the samurai created a unique way of life that emphasised the importance of discipline, honour, and self-control, drawing inspiration from a range of religious traditions to inform their worldview. Their commitment to spiritual cultivation and their focus on living with integrity and purpose continues to inspire us today.

The legacy of the samurai serves as a reminder of the power of spiritual knowledge and the importance of living with intention and purpose. By cultivating inner peace and balance and dedicating themselves to ongoing spiritual practice, the samurai achieved a level of mastery that extended beyond the martial arts and into all aspects of their lives.

The samurai were highly educated and open to new ideas and spiritual influences from a variety of traditions. Their proximity to death and focus on living in the moment led them to value spiritual knowledge and seek wisdom wherever it could be found. The samurai legacy serves as a testament to the power of spiritual cultivation and the importance of living with discipline, honour, and self-control. It continues to inspire us to this day.

"The legacy of the samurai lives on to this day, reminding us of the power of spiritual cultivation and the importance of living with integrity and purpose"

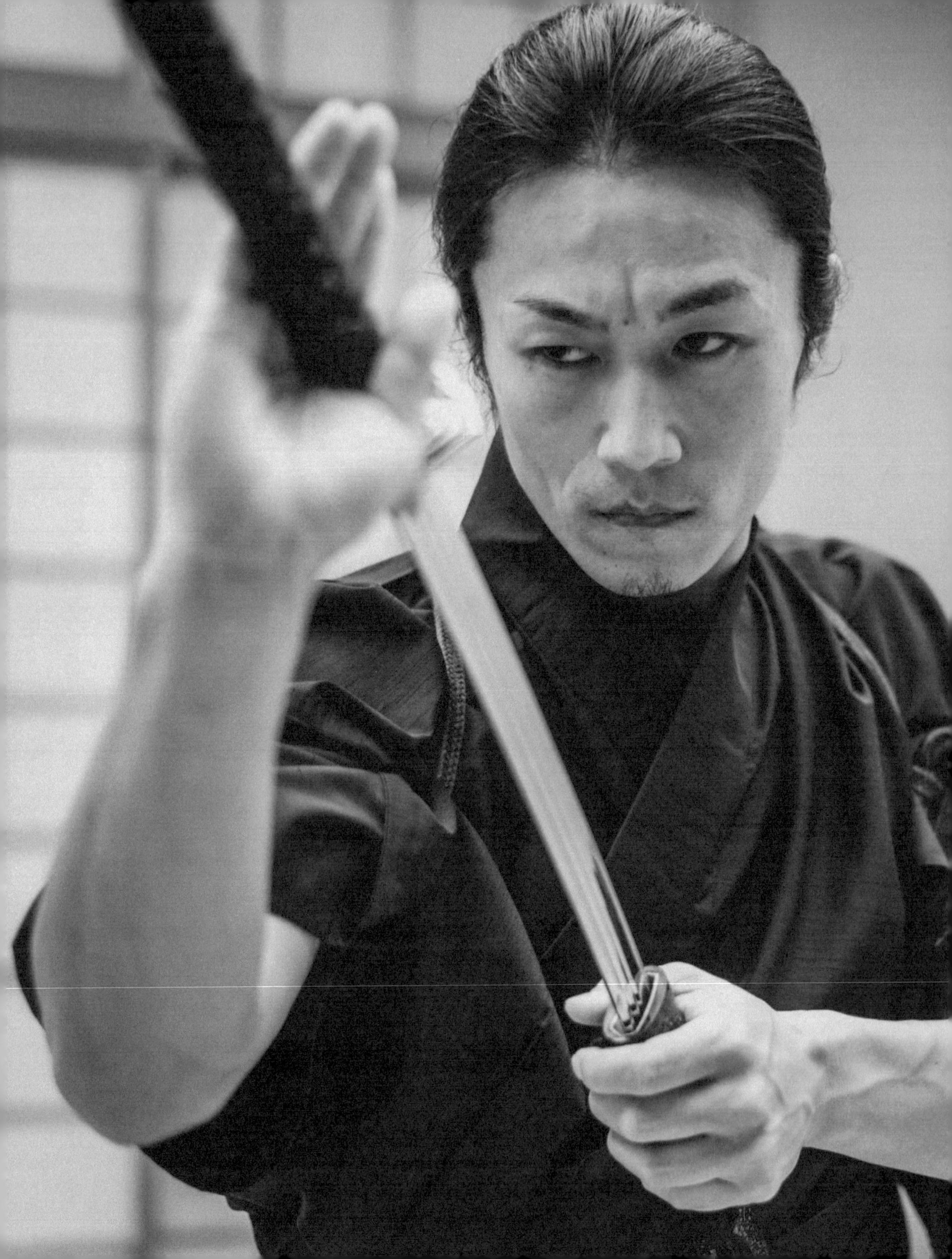

# TRAINING THE SAMURAI

Samurai training encompassed diverse skills, from martial arts and swordsmanship to literature, poetry, calligraphy and politics. Spiritual development was also crucial, with Zen meditation and Shinto rituals used to cultivate mental and emotional discipline. This multifaceted approach aimed to produce elite warriors who were also skilled in governance and deeply appreciated life's spiritual aspects.

Training for the samurai began at a young age and was considered an essential part of their upbringing. From childhood onwards, samurai were taught discipline, loyalty, and martial arts, all of which were necessary for their role as protectors and enforcers of the law. The samurai's training was often rigorous and demanding, but it was seen as an essential preparation for a life of service to their lord and their community.

*"The primary thing when you take a sword in your hands is your intention to cut the enemy, whatever the means. Whenever you parry, hit, spring, strike or touch the enemy's cutting sword, you must cut the enemy in the same movement. It is essential to attain this. If you think only of hitting, springing,*

*striking or touching the enemy, you will not be able actually to cut him,"* wrote Miyamoto Musashi in The Book of Five Rings.

At the beginning of their training, samurai children would be taught the basic skills of swordsmanship and martial arts. According to eye-witness accounts in "The Way of the Samurai: The Legacy of Japan's Warrior Heroes" by Carol Gaskin and Vince Matsuda, this training would begin at a very young age, around 6-7 years old.

They would first learn the basic skills of swordsmanship, including footwork, posture, and striking techniques. As they grew older, they would be trained in more advanced techniques and tactics, including using other weapons such as spears and bows. The training was rigorous and demanding, and the young samurai were expected to practice for several hours each day.

This training was a way of life designed to create a perfect balance between physical strength, mental discipline, and spiritual enlightenment, as explained in "Samurai: The Story of a Warrior Tradition" by Harry Cook. A modern description of samurai training can be found in "Budo Secrets: Teachings of the Martial Arts Masters" by John Stevens, who explains that the training was based on the principle of *shu-ha-ri*, which meant "protect, break, leave." The intense training focused on developing the student's physical, mental, and spiritual aspects."

The samurai's training was not just limited to martial skills, however. They were also taught the art of calligraphy, poetry, and music, as well as the rules of etiquette and protocol. These skills were essential for the samurai's social status and ability to communicate effectively with other members of society.

As society changed, so too did the training of the samurai. During the Edo period (1603-1868), the samurai focused more on intellectual pursuits and less on martial skills. This was due in part to the relative peace and stability of the period, as well as the influence of Confucianism and other philosophical schools of thought.

However, even as the emphasis on martial skills waned, the samurai continued to be trained in the art of the sword. The sword was seen as an extension of the samurai's body and spirit, and mastery of the sword was considered essential for their role as community protectors.

Throughout their lives, the training of the samurai was a constant process. As they aged, they would be expected to pass on their knowledge and skills to younger generations. This helped to ensure the continuity of the samurai tradition and the preservation of their culture and values.

Today, the training of the samurai continues to be an inspiration for many people. While martial arts and sword use are no longer essential skills for modern-day warriors, discipline, loyalty, and service are important in many fields. The samurai's focus on personal development and the pursuit of excellence can be seen in modern-day practices such as mindfulness and self-improvement.

As we can see, the samurai's training was a rigorous and demanding process that began in childhood and continued throughout their lives. While the specifics of their training may have changed over time, the core values of discipline, loyalty, and service remained constant. Today, the legacy of the samurai continues to inspire people around the world, and their values and teachings remain relevant for those seeking to improve themselves and positively impact the world around them.

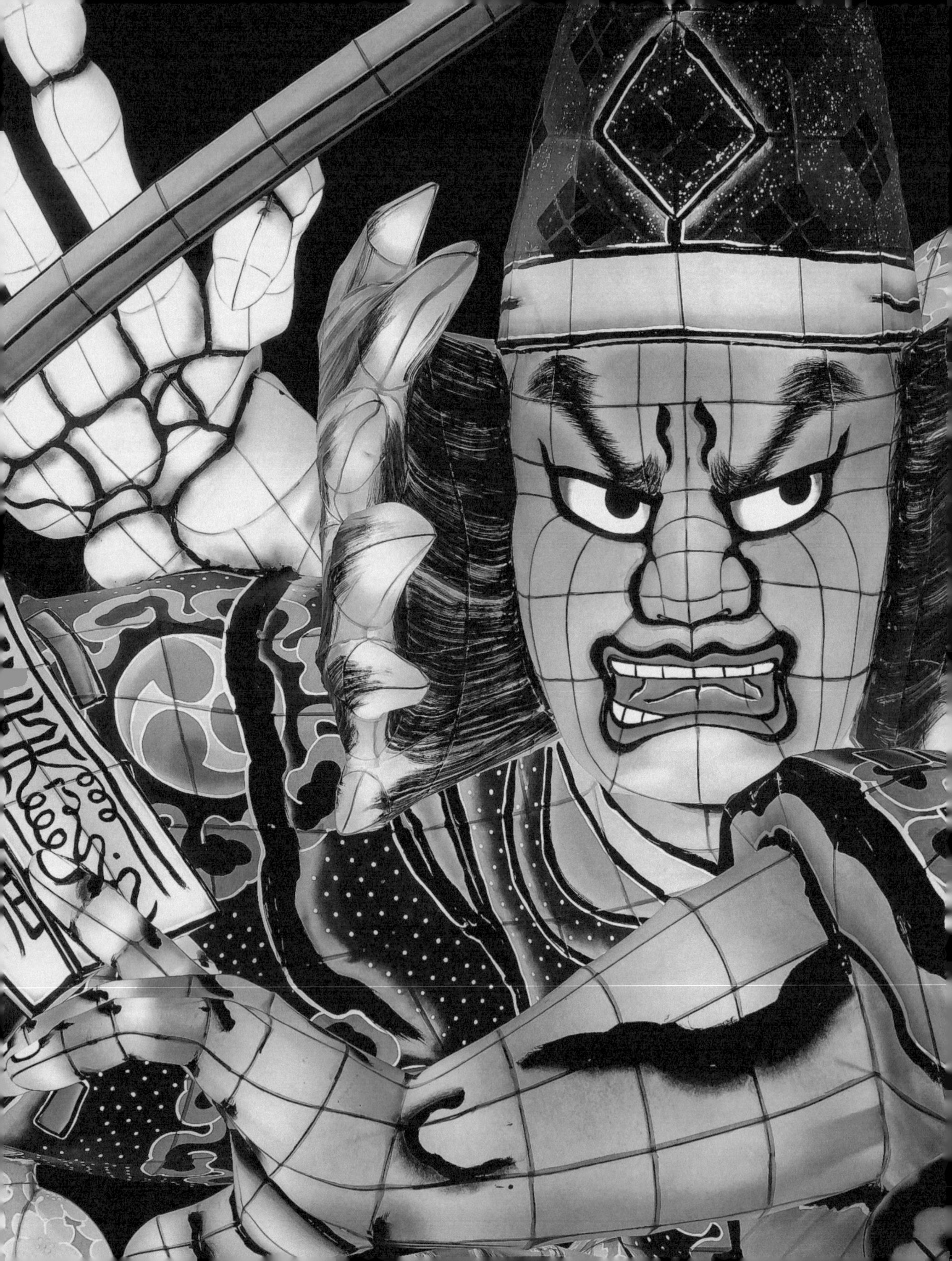

# THE SAMURAI IN POP CULTURE

The samurai remain a popular subject in pop culture due to their captivating values of honour, discipline, and loyalty. While some depictions may oversimplify or exaggerate aspects of their way of life, the enduring appeal of the samurai demonstrates their continued relevance as a symbol of strength and virtue. By embodying these ideals, the samurai continue to inspire and fascinate audiences worldwide.

The samurai have been a fascinating and enduring subject of pop culture for many years. From the early days of Japanese cinema to the explosion of anime and manga in the 21st century, the image of the samurai has captivated audiences around the world. This essay will explore the pop culture representations of the samurai in anime, manga, and video games and analyse what makes them so compelling to fans.

One of the most well-known anime series featuring samurai is Rurouni Kenshin. The story follows a former assassin named Kenshin who, after the Meiji Restoration, has sworn never to kill again and wanders the countryside, helping those in need. The series explores many themes related to the samurai, including Bushido, honour, and the changing times of Japan. Kenshin is an interesting character in that he is a samurai who has forsaken violence, which puts him at odds with other characters in the series who still believe in the old ways of the samurai.

Another popular anime series featuring samurai is Samurai Champloo. This series is set in Edo-period Japan and follows a trio of unlikely heroes: Mugen, a wild and unpredictable swordsman; Jin, a stoic and disciplined samurai; and Fuu, a young girl searching for a samurai who smells of sunflowers. The series is known for its unique blend of hip-hop and samurai culture and action-packed fight scenes. While the series is not strictly historically accurate, it is an entertaining take on the samurai genre.

Manga, the Japanese form of comics, has also produced many memorable stories featuring samurai. One of the most famous is Lone Wolf and Cub, which follows the adventures of Ogami Itto, a disgraced samurai who becomes an assassin for hire with his young son Daigoro. The series is known for its graphic violence, intricate plot, and stunning artwork. It explores themes of revenge, honour, and the bond between father and son. The series has been adapted into several movies and TV shows and has influenced many other works in the samurai genre.

Another popular manga series featuring samurai is Vagabond, which is based on the life of the famous swordsman Miyamoto Musashi. The series follows Musashi's journey from a young, arrogant samurai to a master swordsman and philosopher. The series is known for its realistic portrayal of sword fighting and its deep exploration of the philosophy of Bushido. The series has been praised for its attention to historical detail and its exploration of the human psyche.

In addition to anime and manga, video games have also produced many memorable representations of the samurai. One of the most well-known is the game series Samurai Warriors. This series allows players to take control of famous samurai warriors and battle through historical events of the Sengoku period. The game is known for its intense and satisfying combat and attention to historical detail. It also explores many themes related to the samurai, such as loyalty, honour, and duty.

Another popular video game featuring samurai is Nioh. The game is set in 16th-century Japan and follows the adventures of William Adams, an Englishman who becomes a samurai and fights against demons and supernatural forces. The game is known for its challenging combat, deep customisation options, and its use of historical events and figures. The game explores themes of honour, duty, and the clash of cultures between Japan and the West.

As we can see, the samurai have been a popular subject of pop culture for many years, including in films. Two notable examples of samurai films are "47 Ronin" and "The Last Samurai." Both films take different approaches to portray the samurai and their way of life, and they have generated mixed reactions from fans and critics alike.

"47 Ronin" is a 2013 fantasy action film that stars Keanu Reeves as a half-Japanese, half-British outcast named Kai who helps a group of samurai avenge their master's death. The story is loosely based on the real-life Ako Incident of 1701-1703, in which 47 ronin (samurai without a master) avenged the death of their former lord. The film blends fantasy and Japanese mythology elements and features epic battle scenes and supernatural creatures.

While the film received mixed reviews from critics, it was praised for its visual effects and action sequences. However, it was criticised for its inaccurate portrayal of Japanese culture and history. The film's inclusion of fantasy elements, such as dragons and witches, was seen by some as disrespectful to the true story of the 47 ronin. Additionally, the film's casting of Keanu Reeves as the lead character was controversial, as he is not of Japanese descent.

"The Last Samurai" is a 2003 epic war film that stars Tom Cruise as Nathan Algren, a Civil War veteran hired to train the Japanese army to fight against a samurai rebellion in the late 19th century. The film is set during the Meiji Restoration, a period of rapid modernisation and westernisation in Japan, and explores the clash between traditional Japanese culture and the forces of modernisation. The film featured stunning cinematography and a powerful score and was praised for its attention to detail in recreating the historical setting.

While the film was generally well-received by critics and audiences, it was also criticised for its portrayal of the samurai. Some saw the film as a white saviour narrative, with Tom Cruise's character being seen as the hero who saves the samurai from extinction. Additionally, the film was criticised for portraying the samurai as primitive and backward, depicting their way of life as outdated and ineffective in the face of modern technology.

Overall, both "47 Ronin" and "The Last Samurai" are examples of the ways in which samurai culture has been portrayed in pop culture. While both films have their flaws and inaccuracies, they also offer unique perspectives on the samurai and their way of life. "47 Ronin" takes a more fantastical approach, blending Japanese mythology with the story of the 47 ronin. At the same time, "The Last Samurai" explores the clash between traditional and modern Japan through the eyes of an outsider.

It is worth noting, however, that these films are only a tiny part of the vast and complex history of the samurai. While pop culture representations of the samurai may not always be accurate, they offer a glimpse into the enduring legacy of these legendary warriors.

So what makes these pop culture representations of the samurai so compelling to fans? One reason is the mystique surrounding the samurai. The samurai were a class of warriors who lived by a strict code of honour, and their way of life has been romanticised and mythologised over the years.

Another reason for the enduring appeal of samurai in pop culture is the timeless nature of their stories. While many of these works occur in specific historical periods, the themes and conflicts they explore are universal and timeless. Themes such as honour, loyalty, duty, and the struggle between tradition and progress are all still relevant today and resonate with audiences across cultures and time periods.

Additionally, the samurai's iconic image and distinct style have made them a visual staple in pop culture. The samurai sword, or katana, is instantly recognisable and has become a symbol of the samurai's strength and skill. The samurai's distinctive armour and clothing, with its mix of practicality and style, have also made them popular in cosplay and other forms of fan expression.

However, it is essential to note that many of these pop culture representations of the samurai are not necessarily historically accurate. While some works, like Vagabond and Lone Wolf and Cub, strive for historical authenticity, others take more liberties with the historical record. Samurai Champloo, for example, features anachronistic elements like hip-hop music and modern fashion, while Nioh features supernatural elements and fictional characters. These fictionalised versions of the samurai may not accurately reflect the realities of samurai life, but they still capture the essence of the samurai spirit and mythology.

Undoubtedly, the samurai continue to be a captivating subject in pop culture, appearing in various forms of media such as anime, manga, and video games. These works explore the themes of honour, loyalty, and the struggle between tradition and progress that are still relevant today. While some works strive for historical accuracy, others take more liberties with the historical record, but they still manage to capture the essence of the samurai spirit and mythology.

The enduring appeal of the samurai in pop culture speaks to the universal nature of their stories and their iconic image that continues to fascinate and inspire audiences worldwide.

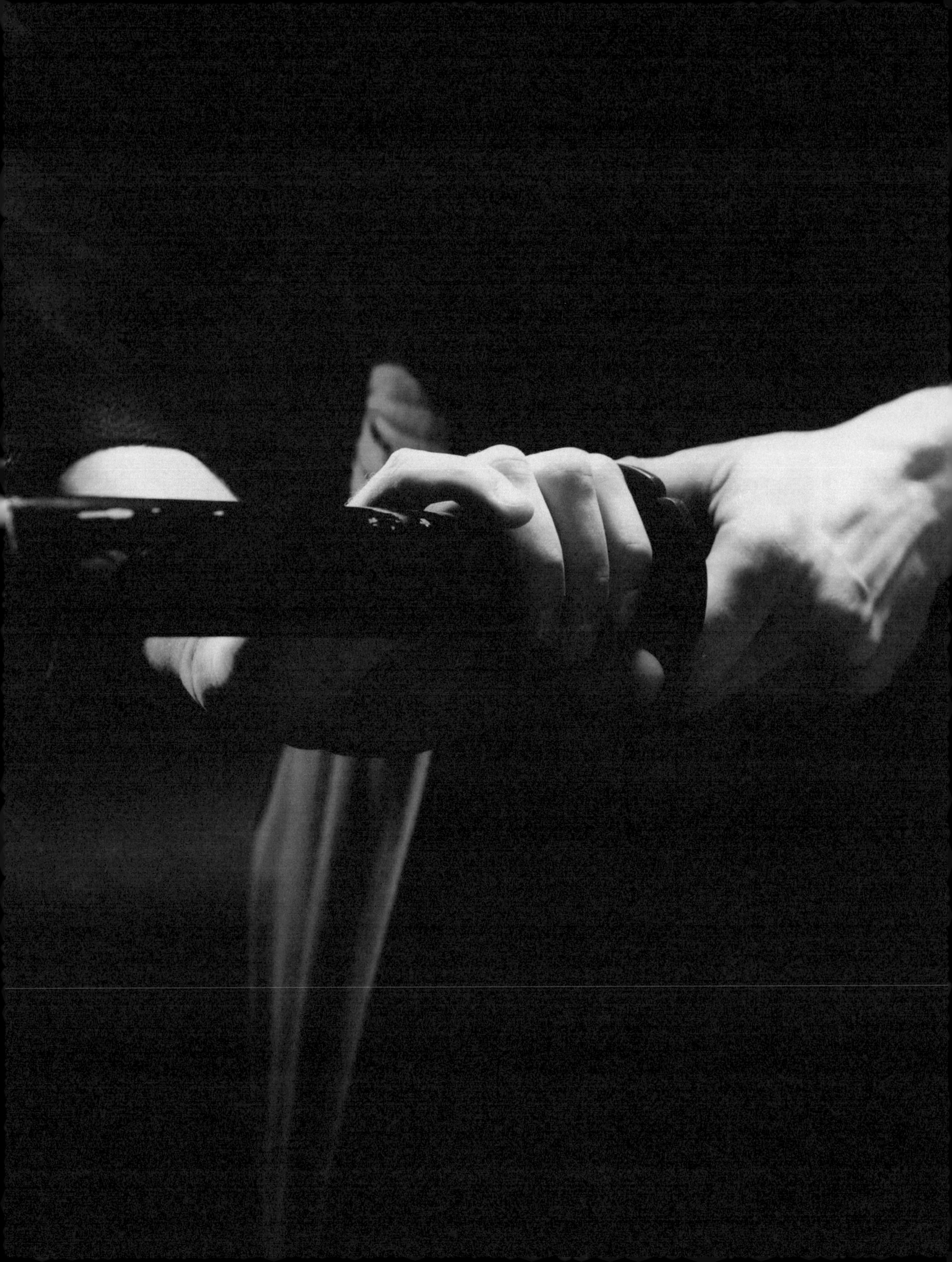

# MEET THE REAL SAMURAI

Contrary to popular belief, the samurai of feudal Japan were not just sword-wielding warriors bound by bushido. They were a diverse group of individuals with a wide range of interests and attitudes, including art, literature, social justice, and gender equality. This chapter explores the multifaceted nature of samurai culture, delving into the lives of eight famous samurai who embody different aspects of this rich and vibrant history. The myth of the western samurai is also challenged, prompting us to question whether anyone outside of Japanese culture can truly be called a samurai.

The samurai of feudal Japan are often portrayed as stoic, sword-wielding warriors who uphold a strict code of honour known as bushido. However, the reality is that the samurai were a diverse group of individuals with a range of attitudes, personalities, and abilities. They were skilled in martial arts, well-educated, and cultured, with interests that extended beyond the battlefield.

Some samurai were renowned for their leadership and strategic prowess, while others excelled as individual warriors. Many were patrons of the arts, fostering cultural activities such as poetry, calligraphy, and tea ceremonies. Women and people of colour also played essential roles in samurai society, with some achieving great acclaim and recognition for their achievements.

Perhaps most strikingly, many samurai held beliefs and attitudes that would not be out of place in the 21st century. Some were advocates of gender equality, while others championed social justice and the rights of the marginalised. Some samurai cross-dressed and challenged gender perceptions. Other Samurai were openly gay or bisexual. Some even went so far as to embrace pacifism, challenging the idea that the only path to honour lay in battle.

In short, the samurai were multifaceted and nuanced individuals who embodied a complex blend of tradition, innovation, and personal expression. They were true renaissance men and women who drew inspiration from bushido and the spirit of the samurai while also forging their own unique paths in life. In this chapter, we will explore the lives and achievements of eight famous samurai, each of whom exemplifies a different facet of this rich and vibrant culture. We will also look at the gender-challenging Onnagata Samurai and those samurai who were gay. And we will examine the myth of the western samurai and ask whether any westerner can ever indeed be called a samurai.

# Yagyu Munenori

## The Legendary Samurai Sword Master

Yagyu Munenori was a samurai swordsman and philosopher living in Japan during the early 17th century. He is renowned for his contributions to the development of martial arts and his teachings on the philosophy of Bushido. Munenori was also an instructor to the Tokugawa shoguns, who were the rulers of Japan at the time.

*"Yagyu Munenori is like a god of martial arts."* - Miyamoto Musashi

*"Yagyu Munenori was the most skilled swordsman of his time."* - Tokugawa Ieyasu

One of the defining qualities of Yagyu Munenori was his commitment to self-control. He believed controlling one's emotions and impulses was the key to success in martial and everyday situations. Munenori emphasised the importance of remaining calm and focused, even in the face of danger or adversity. He believed this was the only way to achieve true mastery in any discipline.

Another essential quality that Munenori emphasised was humility. He believed that arrogance and pride were the downfalls of many warriors and that true strength lay in recognising one's own limitations. Munenori believed that humility was not a sign of weakness but rather a strength that allowed one to learn from others and constantly improve oneself.

Munenori also emphasised the importance of adaptability. He recognised that the world was constantly changing and that those who could not adapt would be left behind. He believed the key to success was learning from experiences and adjusting strategies and techniques accordingly. Munenori's teachings on adaptability are particularly relevant in today's fast-paced and ever-changing world, where the ability to adapt quickly and effectively is often the key to success.

Perhaps one of the most inspiring aspects of Yagyu Munenori's philosophy is his belief in the power of the mind. Munenori believed that the mind was the most potent weapon of all and that the key to success was harnessing its full potential. He emphasised the importance of mental discipline and visualisation and believed that the mind could be trained to achieve almost anything.

*"The true Way of sword fencing is nothing but the mastery of one's own mind."* - Yagyu Munenori

"A warrior, above all, must be a man of wisdom and intellect." - Yagyu Munenori

Munenori's teachings on the power of the mind have been backed up by modern science. Studies have shown that visualisation and mental rehearsal can be as effective as physical practice in improving performance in various domains, including sports, music, and even surgery.

Overall, Yagyu Munenori's philosophy of self-control, humility, adaptability, and the power of the mind is as relevant today as it was in the early 17th century. By adopting Munenori's spirit, we can improve our lives and achieve greater success in all areas.

Firstly, we can learn to manage our emotions and impulses more effectively by cultivating self-control. This can help us to avoid making rash decisions and to stay focused on our goals, even in challenging circumstances. By remaining calm and centred, we can approach problems with a clear mind and make better decisions.

Secondly, by embracing humility, we can learn to recognise our own limitations and seek out the expertise of others. This can help us learn from more experienced people and constantly improve our skills and knowledge.

Thirdly, we can learn to embrace change and adjust our strategies and techniques as needed by developing adaptability. This can help us to stay ahead of the curve in our personal and professional lives and to remain competitive in an ever-changing world.

Finally, by harnessing the power of the mind, we can achieve almost anything we set our minds to. By visualising our goals and practising mental rehearsal, we can improve our performance in various domains and achieve tremendous success in all areas of our lives.

In conclusion, Yagyu Munenori was a true master of martial arts and a philosopher of great insight and wisdom. His teachings on self-control, humility, adaptability, and the power of the mind are as relevant today as they were in the early 17th century. Adopting Munenori's spirit allows us to manage our emotions and impulses more effectively, recognise our limitations, embrace change, and achieve almost anything we set our minds to. Munenori's legacy continues to inspire people worldwide, and his teachings serve as a reminder of the enduring power of Bushido and the importance of living a life of honour and integrity.

# Date Masamune

## The One-Eyed Dragon of Oshu

Date Masamune was a daimyo, or feudal lord, who lived in Japan during the late 16th and early 17th centuries. He was known for his military achievements, patronage of the arts, sense of justice, and commitment to fairness in his dealings with his subjects. Masamune was a complex figure who embodied a range of admirable qualities, and his life and legacy continue to inspire people around the world.

One of the defining qualities of Date Masamune was his military prowess. He was a skilled warrior who led his troops into battle with courage and determination. Masamune was known for his boldness and willingness to take risks to achieve his goals. He was also a skilled strategist who could outmanoeuvre his opponents and secure victories despite overwhelming odds.

*"Date Masamune, the one-eyed dragon of Oshu, was a man of great bravery and ambition. He was a true warrior who lived by the sword and died by the sword. His spirit lives on in the hearts of all who admire the way of the samurai."* Miyamoto Musashi, - The Book of Five Rings

Another essential quality that Masamune embodied was his patronage of the arts. He recognised the importance of culture and the arts in enriching people's lives. Masamune greatly supported traditional Japanese arts such as tea ceremonies, calligraphy, and flower arrangement, and he also supported the development of new art forms such as kabuki theatre.

Masamune was also known for his sense of justice and his commitment to fairness. He believed his duty as a ruler was to ensure that his subjects were treated justly and their rights were protected. Masamune was known for his strict adherence to the law and willingness to hold his own officials accountable for wrongdoing.

Perhaps one of the most inspiring aspects of Date Masamune's character was his commitment to overcoming adversity. Masamune was partially blind in one eye, which made him the subject of ridicule and discrimination from a young age. However, he refused to let this hold him back and instead used his disability as a motivation to achieve greatness. Masamune's determination to succeed despite the obstacles in his path is a powerful reminder of the human capacity for resilience and perseverance.

By adopting Masamune's spirit, we can learn much about how to live our lives more meaningfully and in a fulfilling way. Firstly, by cultivating a sense of courage and determination, we can learn to overcome the obstacles in our own lives and achieve our goals. Masamune's willingness to take risks and his boldness in the face of adversity can inspire those seeking to achieve great things in their own lives.

Secondly, we can enrich our lives and those around us by recognising the importance of culture and the arts. Masamune's patronage of the arts reminds us of the power of beauty and creativity to inspire and lift us.

Thirdly, by committing ourselves to justice and fairness, we can make the world a better place for ourselves and for others. Masamune's sense of duty to his subjects and his commitment to holding his own officials accountable can serve as a model for us as we seek to build a more just and equitable society.

Finally, we can learn to grow and develop by embracing the challenges and obstacles in our lives. Masamune's determination to succeed despite his disability is a testament to the power of resilience and the human spirit to overcome even the most significant challenges.

In conclusion, Date Masamune was a remarkable figure who embodied many admirable qualities. His military prowess, patronage of the arts, sense of justice, and commitment to overcoming adversity continue to inspire people around the world. By adopting Masamune's spirit, we can learn to cultivate courage and determination, appreciate the beauty and creativity of the arts, work towards justice and fairness, and overcome the obstacles in our own lives. Masamune's legacy serves as a powerful reminder of the enduring power of human resilience and the importance of living a life of purpose and meaning. Masamune's life shows us that no matter what obstacles we face, we have the potential to overcome them and achieve greatness if we are willing to work hard and remain committed to our goals.

In addition to his military and cultural achievements, Masamune left a lasting leadership and governance legacy. He was a daimyo who was deeply committed to the well-being of his people, and he worked tirelessly to ensure that they were treated justly and with respect. Masamune's emphasis on fairness and justice in his dealings with his subjects serves as a powerful reminder of the importance of strong leadership in building a better world.

In today's rapidly changing and uncertain world, we can all benefit from the example set by Date Masamune. By embracing his spirit of courage, determination, creativity, justice, and resilience, we can learn to live our own lives with greater purpose and meaning. Whether we are facing personal challenges, striving to achieve our goals, or working to make the world a better place, Masamune's legacy can serve as a guiding light to inspire us on our journey.

# Miyamoto Musashi

## The Undefeated Samurai

Miyamoto Musashi is widely regarded as one of the greatest swordsmen in Japanese history. He is also known as a philosopher, writer, and artist, and his life and teachings continue to inspire people worldwide today. Musashi's spirit of self-discipline, dedication, and mastery can offer valuable lessons for anyone seeking to achieve excellence in their own lives.

*"It is said that Musashi never lost a duel in his lifetime."* The Lone Samurai: The Life of Miyamoto Musashi" by William Scott Wilson

Musashi was born in 1584, and his early life was marked by turmoil and instability. His father was a samurai, but he abandoned the family when Musashi was young, leaving him to be raised by his mother and uncle. Musashi became a skilled swordsman as a young man, but he was also known for his impulsive and reckless behaviour.

In his mid-twenties, Musashi began a period of intense self-reflection and study that would shape the rest of his life. He spent years travelling throughout Japan, engaging in duels and battles with other swordsmen, and developing his own unique style of fighting. Along the way, he also wrote several books, including the famous "Book of Five Rings," which is still widely read and studied today.

A relentless focus on self-improvement and mastery characterises Musashi's life and teachings. He believed that true excellence could only be achieved through hard work, discipline, and a deep understanding of oneself and one's opponents. Musashi was known for strictly adhering to his personal code of ethics, emphasising honesty, integrity, and loyalty.

*"The way of the sword and the way of Zen are identical, for they have the same purpose; that of killing the ego."* The Book of Five Rings

One of the critical lessons we can learn from Musashi is the importance of self-discipline and dedication. Musashi's success as a swordsman was not simply the result of his natural talent or physical ability but rather his unwavering commitment to mastering his craft. By setting clear goals and working tirelessly to achieve them, Musashi attained a level of skill and expertise that few others have ever matched.

Another important lesson we can learn from Musashi is the importance of self-awareness and mindfulness. Musashi believed that true mastery required a deep understanding of oneself, including one's strengths and weaknesses, and a deep appreciation of one's opponents. By staying focused and present in the moment, Musashi achieved a level of mental clarity and sharpness that allowed him to outmanoeuvre even the most skilled opponents.

*"Perceive that which cannot be seen with the eye,"*

Musashi's teachings also offer valuable lessons for anyone seeking to live a life of purpose and meaning. By emphasising the importance of integrity, loyalty, and honesty, Musashi reminds us that our actions have consequences and that we should always strive to do the right thing, even in the face of adversity. His commitment to excellence and dedication to his craft serve as a potent reminder that we all have the potential to achieve great things if we are willing to put in the work and stay focused on our goals.

In today's fast-paced and constantly changing world, Miyamoto Musashi's teachings can offer valuable insights into how we can live our lives with greater purpose and meaning. By adopting his spirit of self-discipline, dedication, and mastery, we can learn to achieve excellence in our lives and become the best version of ourselves.

Whether we are seeking to improve our skills, deepen our relationships, or find greater meaning and purpose in our work, Musashi's legacy can inspire us to reach new heights and achieve our full potential.

# Takeda Shingen

## The Legendary Tiger of Kai

Takeda Shingen was a powerful daimyo and military strategist living in Japan during the late 16th century. He was known for his brilliant military campaigns and leadership skills, which have earned him a reputation as one of the greatest military commanders in Japanese history. Shingen's unwavering commitment to preparation, strategy, and leadership offers valuable lessons for anyone seeking to achieve success in their own lives.

Shingen was born in 1521, and from an early age, he displayed a talent for leadership and strategic thinking. As he grew older, he became increasingly interested in military matters and became a skilled warrior and tactician. Shingen was also known for his strict discipline and high standards, and he demanded the same level of dedication and excellence from his soldiers.

One of the key qualities that set Shingen apart was his emphasis on preparation and strategy. Shingen believed that success in battle was not just a matter of skill or bravery but also a matter of careful planning and preparation.

*"The enemy is always stronger in imagination than in reality."* - Takeda Shingen

He was known for his meticulous attention to detail, and he would often spend months or even years preparing for a single battle.

*"In strategy, it is important to see distant things as if they were close and to take a distanced view of close things."* - Takeda Shingen

Another important quality that Shingen possessed was his ability to inspire and lead others. He was respected by his allies and enemies alike and had a talent for bringing out the best in his soldiers. Shingen understood that leadership was not only about giving orders but also about building solid relationships and inspiring others to achieve their full potential.

Shingen's life and teachings offer valuable lessons for anyone seeking to achieve success in their own lives. His emphasis on preparation and strategy serves as a reminder that success is not just a matter of luck or natural ability but also a matter of careful planning and hard work. By preparing for our goals and thinking strategically about achieving them, we can increase our chances of success and minimise the risks of failure.

Shingen's emphasis on leadership and inspiration also offers valuable lessons for anyone seeking to lead others. By setting high standards and demanding excellence, while also inspiring and supporting others, we can build strong and effective teams that are capable of achieving great things. Shingen's leadership style serves as a reminder that authentic leadership is not just about giving orders but also about building strong relationships and inspiring others to be their best selves.

Finally, Shingen's unwavering commitment to his own principles and beliefs serves as an inspiration to us all. Shingen remained true to his values and beliefs throughout his life, even in the face of adversity. His commitment to excellence and his dedication to his soldiers are potent reminders that we can all achieve great things if we remain true to our principles and beliefs.

Takeda Shingen's commitment to his Confucian principles and beliefs was a defining aspect of his character and leadership style. He believed that the principles of Confucianism, such as filial piety, loyalty, and moral integrity, were essential for building a solid and stable society. Shingen saw himself as a protector of these values and worked tirelessly to instil them in his soldiers and the people under his rule.

One of the core tenets of Confucianism is the idea of the "superior man," a person who embodies the highest ideals of morality and wisdom. Shingen saw himself as a superior man, and he strove to embody these ideals in his daily life. He was known for his strict discipline and high moral standards, demanding the same level of excellence from his soldiers. Shingen believed that by setting a positive example and demonstrating the principles of Confucianism in his own life, he could inspire others to do the same.

*"The warrior's code is eternal. It does not change with the times or the era."* - Takeda Shingen

Another fundamental principle of Confucianism is the importance of education and self-cultivation. Shingen firmly believed in the value of education and encouraged his soldiers and officials to study literature, philosophy, and other subjects that would broaden their understanding of the world. He also believed in the importance of self-cultivation, or the process of refining one's own character and behaviour. Shingen believed that he could become a better leader and set a positive example for his followers by focusing on self-cultivation.

Shingen's adherence to Confucian principles also influenced his approach to governance. He believed that rulers had a responsibility to serve the people under their rule and to promote their welfare. Shingen was known for his fair and just governance and worked hard to ensure his subjects were treated respectfully and with dignity. He also believed in the importance of social order and stability and worked tirelessly to maintain a strong and stable society.

*"In governing men and serving heaven, there is nothing like moderation."* - Takeda Shingen

In conclusion, Takeda Shingen's adherence to Confucian principles was a defining aspect of his character and leadership style. He believed that the principles of Confucianism were essential for building a strong and stable society, and he worked tirelessly to instil these values in his soldiers and the people under his rule. By embodying the ideals of the "superior man," emphasising education and self-cultivation, and promoting fair and just governance, Shingen set a positive example for others to follow and left an enduring legacy in Japanese history.

.

# Yasuke

## The African Samurai

Yasuke was an enslaved African who became one of Japan's most famous black samurai. Although little is known about his early life, it is believed that he was born in Mozambique in the late 16th century and was brought to Japan as a servant of the Jesuit missionary Alessandro Valignano. When Valignano arrived in Japan in 1579, he brought Yasuke with him as his personal servant. During this time, Yasuke first caught the attention of the powerful daimyo Oda Nobunaga.

Nobunaga was one of the most powerful warlords in Japan at the time, and he was known for his military prowess and his innovative tactics. When he saw Yasuke for the first time, he was reportedly amazed by the man's size and strength, and he immediately took him on as a retainer. Yasuke quickly proved himself as a skilled fighter and was soon given a position as one of Nobunaga's personal bodyguards.

One account from a contemporary of Yasuke's is from the Jesuit missionary Luis Frois, who wrote about Yasuke in his historical account of Japan. Frois wrote about Yasuke's arrival in Japan with Alessandro Valignano and his subsequent service to Oda Nobunaga, describing Yasuke as *"black as an ox, tall as a tree, and possessed of the strength of ten men."* This description highlights the physical attributes that made Yasuke stand out in Japan and his strength and skill as a warrior.

Yasuke was not just an imposing physical specimen, however. He was also known for his intelligence and his ability to adapt to Japanese culture. Although initially treated as an outsider due to his skin colour, he quickly learned to speak Japanese and adhere to Japanese customs and etiquette. He was even given his own set of samurai armour, which he wore proudly as a symbol of his new status.

Another account is from the 17th-century Japanese historian Arai Hakuseki, who wrote about Yasuke in his book *Chronicle of Lord Nobunaga*. In it, he described Yasuke as having *"skin black like that of an ox"* but also noted his impressive physical strength and proficiency in Japanese. This description emphasises the challenges that Yasuke faced as a foreigner in Japan but also acknowledges his ability to adapt to Japanese culture and become a skilled samurai.

Yasuke fought alongside Nobunaga in several battles, including the famous Battle of Tenmokuzan, in which Nobunaga defeated the powerful daimyo Takeda Katsuyori. Yasuke's role in the battle is not well-documented, but it is believed that he fought bravely alongside his fellow samurai.

Despite his success as a samurai, Yasuke's time in Japan was short-lived. After Nobunaga died in 1582, Yasuke left Japan and returned to his homeland. Little is known about the rest of his life. Still, he is believed to have returned to the Jesuits and served as a missionary in India before disappearing from historical records.

Yasuke's story is inspiring because of his status as a black samurai and his ability to adapt and excel in a foreign culture. He rose above the prejudices of his time and became a respected member of Japanese society, thanks to his intelligence, strength, and commitment to the samurai way of life.

Yasuke's story also highlights that the samurai were not just a homogenous group of warriors but a diverse collection of individuals from different backgrounds and life experiences. While Yasuke was undoubtedly an unusual figure in Japanese society, his story reminds us that many others like him were able to carve out a place for themselves in the samurai world.

Ultimately, Yasuke's story serves as a reminder that greatness can come from unexpected places. Despite his humble origins and the barriers he faced, Yasuke rose to the highest levels of Japanese society and became a symbol of strength, courage, and determination. His story should inspire us all to strive for greatness, no matter our obstacles.

# Nakano Takeko

## The Fearless Onna-Bugeisha

Nakano Takeko was a samurai warrior living in Japan during the late 19th century. She was born in 1847 in Edo, which is now modern-day Tokyo. Nakano was born into the Aizu clan, a powerful samurai clan with a long tradition of training women in the martial arts.

At a young age, Nakano began training in martial arts, including archery, swordsmanship, and the naginata, a long polearm weapon. She quickly became skilled in these arts, and her talent did not go unnoticed.

In 1868, a conflict known as the Boshin War broke out in Japan. The war pitted the supporters of the Tokugawa shogunate against those who wanted to restore imperial rule to Japan. The Aizu clan sided with the shogunate, and Nakano joined the fight as a member of the Joshitai, a unit of female warriors trained by the Aizu clan.

Nakano quickly distinguished herself as a skilled warrior and leader. She was appointed as the leader of the Joshitai, and her unit fought bravely in several battles against the imperial forces. Nakano was known for her skill with the naginata, and she was able to use it to significant effect in combat.

*"Nakano Takeko was a true warrior, both skilled and courageous. Her leadership of the Joshitai during the Battle of Aizu is a testament to her abilities and her commitment to her clan."* - The Samurai Way: The Life and Legacy of Nakano Takeko by Hiroshi Nakamura

One of the most famous battles in which Nakano fought was the Battle of Aizu, which took place in October 1868. In this battle, the imperial forces attacked the city of Aizu, which was defended by the Aizu clan and their allies. Nakano and her unit of female warriors fought bravely in the battle, and they could hold off the enemy for some time.

However, as the battle turned against them, Nakano knew defeat was inevitable. Rather than be captured by the enemy, Nakano ordered one of her followers to behead her. Legend has it that she made this decision because she did not want to be taken captive and humiliated and because she wanted to die with honour.

*"Nakano Takeko's sacrifice embodies the samurai code of bushido, which emphasises honour and loyalty above all else. Her death was a tragic loss for her clan, but it also served as a powerful example of courage and selflessness."* - Women Warriors: An Illustrated History by David E. Jones

Nakano's sacrifice has made her a legendary figure in Japanese history. She is remembered as a symbol of female strength and courage, and her story has inspired countless people in Japan and worldwide.

Nakano's life and legacy serve as a reminder that women have played an important role in Japanese history and that their contributions should not be overlooked or forgotten. Her story shows that women can be just as brave and capable as men and have the potential to be great leaders and warriors.

*"Nakano Takeko's legacy is a reminder that women have always been a part of Japan's martial traditions, even if their contributions have often been overlooked or forgotten. Her story is an inspiration to women everywhere who aspire to be strong and courageous."* - Samurai Women by Stephen Turnbull

Today, Nakano is remembered as a hero and a symbol of courage and honour. Her legacy lives on through the stories and legends that have been passed down through the generations, and she continues to inspire people to this day. Nakano Takeko is a true inspiration to all who hear her story, and her spirit of bravery and determination serves as a shining example for us all.

# Tsunenaga Hasekura

## The Christian Samurai

Tsunenaga Hasekura was a samurai who defied conventions and took a unique path in his life, leading him to explore foreign lands and cultures. Born in 1571 in the Sendai domain of Japan, Hasekura was a noble family member serving the powerful Date clan. From a young age, he received a thorough education in the martial arts, literature, and calligraphy and quickly became known for his leadership and diplomatic skills.

What sets Hasekura apart from other samurai of his time is his conversion to Christianity, a relatively new and controversial religion in Japan at the time. Hasekura was introduced to Christianity by Spanish missionaries who had arrived in Japan in the late 16th century. Intrigued by the teachings of the religion, Hasekura decided to convert and become a Christian himself, even though most samurai at the time followed traditional Shinto and Buddhist practices.

Hasekura's conversion to Christianity did not go unnoticed by his superiors, but it did not hinder his rise to prominence within the Date clan. In fact, his knowledge of foreign languages and his diplomatic skills made him a valuable asset to the clan, and he was chosen to lead an official delegation to Europe in 1613. The delegation's mission was to establish trade relations with European countries and to secure allies and support for Japan's political and military goals.

Hasekura and his delegation sailed from Japan to Mexico, where they were received by Spanish authorities who were impressed by Hasekura's command of Spanish and his knowledge of European customs and politics. From Mexico, the delegation continued to Spain, where they met with King Philip III and were granted an audience with the Pope in Rome. Hasekura's diplomatic skills were tested as he negotiated trade agreements and exchanged gifts with European leaders, all while navigating the time's complex political and religious landscape.

Hasekura's journey to Europe was not without its challenges and setbacks. The delegation faced hostility and suspicion from some European officials who viewed them as exotic curiosities rather than serious negotiators. Hasekura also encountered resistance from some members of the Japanese nobility, who considered his conversion to Christianity a betrayal of Japanese culture and traditions.

Despite these obstacles, Hasekura remained committed to his mission and his faith. His journey to Europe gave him a unique perspective on the world and its many cultures, and he returned to Japan with a wealth of knowledge and experiences that he used to further the interests of his clan and his country. Hasekura's legacy as a samurai who defied convention and sought to bridge cultural divides has inspired many in Japan and beyond.

The story of Tsunenaga Hasekura is an inspiring one, not just for his bravery and leadership skills but also for his willingness to explore new ideas and cultures. His conversion to Christianity and his travels to Europe were unprecedented for a samurai of his time, and his achievements paved the way for greater understanding and cooperation between Japan and the Western world. Hasekura's example shows us that, even in a world where conformity is valued above all else, it is possible to chart a new course and pursue one's own unique path. His legacy inspires those seeking to break down barriers and forge connections between cultures and people.

*"Hasekura's journey to Europe was an extraordinary feat of diplomacy and cultural exchange, and one that would leave a lasting impression on both Japan and Europe."* - David Howell, Professor of Japanese History at Harvard University.

*"Hasekura was a remarkable figure who defied convention and challenged the status quo. His journey to Europe was a testament to his courage and leadership, and his legacy continues to inspire us to this day."* - Junichi Miyashita, Professor of History at Waseda University in Tokyo.

*"Hasekura's conversion to Christianity was a bold move that set him apart from his fellow samurai. His travels to Europe gave him a unique perspective on the world, and he used his knowledge to promote trade and cooperation between Japan and Europe."* - Keiko McDonald, Professor Emeritus of Japanese Literature at the University of Pittsburgh.

# Sakamoto Ryoma

## The Freedom Fighter

Sakamoto Ryoma was a samurai who challenged the norms of his time and believed in personal freedom and individual rights. He was born in 1836 in the Tosa Domain, now part of present-day Kochi Prefecture in Japan. His family was not wealthy, and

Ryoma grew up with a deep sense of social justice and a desire to make a difference in the world.

Ryoma became involved in politics at a young age, and the ideas of western democracy and freedom profoundly influenced him. He believed that Japan needed to modernise and establish a new, democratic government that would represent the interests of all its citizens, not just the ruling samurai class. Ryoma's ideas were radical for his time, as the traditional samurai values emphasised loyalty to one's lord and adherence to hierarchy and social order.

*"If we cannot abolish the feudal system altogether, we can at least make it more just and humane."* - Sakamoto Ryoma

In 1854, when Ryoma was 18, he joined the Tosa Loyalist Party, a group of samurai working to restore power to the emperor and overthrow the Tokugawa shogunate. The shogunate had been in power for over 200 years and had become corrupt and stagnant. Ryoma was a talented strategist and quickly rose through the ranks of the Tosa Loyalist Party. He was known for his ability to bridge the gap between different factions within the party and bring them together towards a common goal.

*"Ryoma was a genius at uniting different factions."* - Yamauchi Yodo, a contemporary of Sakamoto Ryoma

In 1867, Ryoma was pivotal in establishing the Satsuma-Choshu Alliance, a coalition between two powerful samurai domains that helped overthrow the shogunate and establish a new, modern government in Japan. Ryoma was a crucial figure in the negotiations between the Satsuma and Choshu domains, and his diplomatic skills were instrumental in bringing the two sides together.

*"Ryoma is the pillar of our revolution."* - Saigo Takemori, a prominent figure in the Meiji Restoration

Ryoma's ideas and actions were truly revolutionary for his time, as he challenged the traditional samurai values of loyalty, hierarchy, and social order. He believed in personal freedom and individual rights and was unafraid to speak out against injustice and oppression. His vision for a new, modern Japan that embraced western ideas of democracy and freedom was truly ahead of its time.

Ryoma's legacy continues to inspire people today, and his ideas about personal freedom and individual rights are just as relevant in modern society as they were in his time. In today's world, we are still grappling with social justice and inequality issues, and the importance of personal freedom and individual rights is just as pressing as ever.

*"Ryoma was a great man of integrity and courage."* - Shiba Ryotaro

Ryoma's example shows us that it is possible to challenge the status quo and fight for what we believe in, even in the face of adversity and opposition. His commitment to his ideals and his willingness to take risks in pursuit of his goals are truly inspiring, and they remind us that change is possible, even in the most difficult of circumstances.

*"Ryoma was a visionary who saw a better future for Japan."* - Donald Keene, scholar of Japanese literature and culture

In conclusion, Sakamoto Ryoma was an unconventional samurai who challenged traditional values and beliefs and believed in personal freedom and individual rights. His legacy continues to inspire people today, and his ideas about democracy and freedom are just as relevant in modern society as they were in his time. Ryoma's example reminds us that it is possible to effect change and fight for what we believe in, even in the face of adversity and opposition.

# Onnagata Samurai

## The Gender-Challenging Samurai

The samurai were known for their strict adherence to a code of honour and social norms that governed all aspects of their lives. One of the most important of these norms was the strict division of roles between men and women, which dictated that women were to be subservient to men in all aspects of life. However, not all samurai adhered to these gender roles, and some even challenged them outright.

One group of samurai who challenged traditional gender roles were the "onnagata" performers of Kabuki theatre. Kabuki is a traditional form of Japanese theatre that dates back to the 17th century. It is known for its elaborate costumes, stylized movements, and melodramatic plots. In Kabuki, all roles, including those of female characters, were traditionally played by male actors. However, within the world of Kabuki, there was a subcategory of male actors who specialised in playing female roles, known as onnagata.

*"The onnagata is the foundation of Kabuki. Without the onnagata, there would be no Kabuki."* - Nakamura Ganjiro I, a Kabuki actor and onnagata performer.

The onnagata samurai were often seen as subversive and controversial within samurai society. They challenged the rigid gender roles that governed all aspects of samurai life, including the roles men and women were expected to play in the theatre. The onnagata performers were able to portray female characters in a convincing and captivating way, and they quickly became some of the most popular and respected performers in the Kabuki tradition.

*"The onnagata were both subversive and popular. They challenged the rigid gender roles of samurai society and brought new life to the theatre."* - Carol Fisher Sorgenfrei, Unspeakable Acts: The Avant-garde Theatre of Terayama Shuji and Post-war Japan.

*"The onnagata performer was the epitome of beauty and elegance. They were able to capture the essence of femininity in a way that was both convincing and captivating."* - Zoë Kincaid. Kabuki: The Popular Stage of Japan"

Despite the controversy surrounding the onnagata samurai, they were widely admired for their skill and artistry. They were known for their ability to portray the full range of human emotions and experiences, from love and longing to jealousy and revenge. They were also respected for their ability to push the boundaries of traditional gender roles and challenge the status quo.

*"The onnagata performer was not merely a man playing a woman's role, but a unique entity unto themselves, an onnagata."* - James R. Brandon. Kabuki Heroes on the Osaka Stage 1780-1830

The onnagata samurai were not the only samurai to challenge traditional gender roles. There were also women samurai, known as *onna-bugeisha*, who were trained in martial arts and fought alongside their male counterparts in battle. While women samurai were relatively rare, they were a testament to the fact that samurai society was not as rigidly divided along gender lines as some might think.

The onnagata samurai and the onna-bugeisha represent two very different challenges to traditional gender roles within samurai society. The onnagata performers challenged traditional gender roles through their art by portraying female characters convincingly and captivatingly. The onna-bugeisha, on the other hand, challenged conventional gender roles through their actions by taking up arms and fighting alongside their male counterparts in battle.

In many ways, the onnagata samurai and the onna-bugeisha can be seen as precursors to modern-day challenges to traditional gender roles and expectations. Today, many people are challenging traditional notions of gender and masculinity and are pushing for greater acceptance of non-traditional gender identities and expressions. While the onnagata samurai and the onna-bugeisha were undoubtedly not the first to challenge traditional gender roles, they were pioneers in their own right. Their legacy lives on today in the ongoing struggle for gender equality and acceptance.

In conclusion, the onnagata samurai represents an important and often overlooked chapter in the history of samurai society. These subversive performers challenged traditional gender roles and expectations through their art and helped to pave the way for greater acceptance of non-traditional gender identities and expressions. While the onnagata samurai were undoubtedly not the only samurai to challenge traditional gender roles, they are an inspiring reminder that even in the most rigidly structured societies, there is always the potential for change and growth.

# The Gay Samurai

Homosexuality and same-sex relationships have been a part of Japanese culture for centuries, and the samurai period (1185-1868) was no exception. While it is difficult to determine the exact prevalence of same-sex relationships among samurai, numerous historical records and cultural artefacts suggest that homosexuality was not uncommon in this period.

It is important to note that same-sex relationships' cultural and social context in samurai society differed significantly from that of modern Western society. Same-sex relationships were not defined in terms of sexual orientation or identity but rather in terms of social and cultural roles. Specific terms were used to describe same-sex relationships, such as *nanshoku* (male-male love) and *onna-do* (womanly way), which referred to specific social and cultural roles rather than sexual orientation.

Within samurai society, same-sex relationships were often seen as an extension of the mentor-student relationship. Younger samurai often formed intimate relationships with their more experienced and established counterparts, who would act as mentors and teachers in martial and cultural arts. These relationships were often seen as a way to learn from more experienced samurai and gain knowledge and skills necessary for success in samurai society.

*"In samurai society, same-sex relationships were not seen as taboo or shameful. They were viewed as a natural extension of the close relationships that were formed between mentor and student."* - The Samurai: A Military History

In addition to the mentor-student relationship, same-sex relationships were also present among male and female geishas, who were highly trained entertainers and often formed intimate relationships with their clients. It was not uncommon for samurai to patronise geishas, and same-sex relationships between samurai and geishas were not unheard of.

*"Geishas were not just entertainers, they were also highly skilled in conversation, art, and music. It is no surprise that samurai were drawn to them, and that same-sex relationships were formed between them."* - Lesley Downer. Geisha: The Secret History of a Vanishing World

There are also numerous historical records of openly gay samurai. One famous example is the samurai warrior Minamoto no Yoshitsune, who lived during the 12th century and was known for his close relationship with his male retainer, Musashibo Benkei. According to historical records, Yoshitsune and Benkei were inseparable and shared a deep bond that extended beyond the bounds of a typical mentor-student relationship.

Another example is the samurai lord Oda Nobunaga, who lived during the late 16th century and was known for his unconventional and progressive ideas. It is said that Nobunaga was openly bisexual and had both male and female lovers.

*"Oda Nobunaga was known for his progressive ideas and unconventional behaviour, and his same-sex relationships were just one example of this. He was a man ahead of his time."* - Mark Ravina, "The Last Samurai: The Life and Battles of Saigo Takamori"

Despite the presence of same-sex relationships in samurai society, it is essential to note that these relationships were not universally accepted or condoned. While some samurai saw same-sex relationships as a natural and normal part of samurai culture, others viewed them as immoral or unnatural. Sometimes, same-sex relationships could lead to social ostracism or even death, depending on the specific circumstances.

The cultural and social context of same-sex relationships in Japan has evolved significantly. While same-sex marriage is not currently legal in Japan, there is a growing movement to recognise and support the rights of the LGBTQ+ community. This movement has been partly driven by increasing awareness of the historical presence of same-sex relationships in Japanese culture, including samurai society.

In conclusion, while same-sex relationships were not uncommon in samurai society, the cultural and social context of these relationships differed significantly from that of modern Western culture. Same-sex relationships were often viewed as an extension of the mentor-student relationship or as a part of the geisha-client relationship. While some samurai saw same-sex relationships as a natural and normal part of samurai culture, others viewed them as immoral or unnatural. Today, the cultural and social context of same-sex relationships in Japan has evolved significantly, and there is a growing movement to recognise and support the rights of the LGBTQ+ community.

# The Reality of the Western Samurai

The concept of a "western samurai" is a complex and controversial one, as it combines elements of both Japanese and Western cultures. While it is true that some Westerners did become involved in the samurai way of life during the late 19th century, the idea of a Westerner becoming a samurai in the traditional sense is largely a work of fiction.

*"The idea of a Westerner becoming a samurai is a romantic notion that has little basis in reality,"* said Dr Stephen Turnbull, historian and author. *"While there were certainly foreigners who dabbled in samurai culture during the Meiji period, they were never fully accepted as samurai in the traditional sense."*

The character portrayed by Tom Cruise in the film "The Last Samurai" is based loosely on the historical figure of Jules Brunet, a French military officer who became involved in the Satsuma Rebellion of 1877, a conflict between the Japanese government and rebel samurai who opposed the modernisation of Japan. While Brunet did fight alongside the rebels and was briefly honoured as a samurai, he was not entirely accepted into the samurai class and returned to France after the rebellion was suppressed.

The historical context of Japan during the late 19th century was a time of significant change and upheaval. After centuries of isolation, Japan opened its doors to the world, and Western influence rapidly transformed the country. The samurai class, the ruling elite for centuries, faced new challenges and opportunities as their traditional way of life was being threatened by modernisation and Westernisation.

The Satsuma Rebellion of 1877, which lasted from January to September, was a significant event during a period of change in Japan. The rebellion was led by Saigo Takamori, a former samurai who had become disillusioned with the modernising policies of the Japanese government. Saigo and his followers, many of whom were also samurai from the Satsuma domain, rose against the government and fought for several months before being defeated.

The causes of the rebellion can be traced back to the Meiji Restoration of 1868, which saw the end of the samurai class and the beginning of a new era of modernisation in Japan. Many samurai, including Saigo Takamori, were unhappy with the new order and felt that their way of life was being threatened. Additionally, the government's conscription and taxation policies were unpopular, particularly in the Satsuma domain, which had a long history of rebellion against the central government.

According to historian and author Dr Thomas Conlan, *"The Satsuma Rebellion was a time of great upheaval in Japan. The samurai, who had been the ruling class for centuries, were facing new challenges and opportunities as Japan rapidly modernised. The rebellion was a last gasp of resistance against the new order."*

During the Satsuma Rebellion, Jules Brunet, a French military advisor, became involved with the rebel samurai. Brunet and a small group of other Westerners, primarily military advisors, fought alongside the samurai in what was a controversial move. Many Japanese saw their involvement as unwanted foreign interference in a domestic conflict. However, Brunet and his companions fought bravely and were ultimately praised for their dedication to the samurai cause. Brunet was even awarded the title of samurai by Saigo Takamori himself, a rare honour for a foreigner.

However, it is important to note that while Brunet was briefly accepted as a samurai, he was never fully integrated into the samurai class. His position was unique and somewhat precarious, and he eventually returned to France after the rebellion was put down.

Clearly, the concept of a "western samurai" is essentially a work of fiction. While there were undoubtedly Westerners who became involved in Japanese culture and even samurai culture during this period, they were not fully accepted as samurai in the traditional sense. Samurai society was built around strict hierarchies and a deep understanding of cultural identity. It would have been difficult for an outsider to integrate into this way of life fully.

Additionally, the concept of a Westerner becoming a samurai raises questions about cultural appropriation and the commodification of Japanese culture. The samurai are a powerful symbol of Japanese identity and culture. The idea of a non-Japanese person becoming a samurai can be seen as a disrespectful or even offensive distortion of this symbol.

However, it is worth noting that blending different cultures can also be a positive process. The history of Japan is filled with examples of cultural exchange and hybridisation, and the influence of Western culture on Japan during the late 19th century was a significant turning point in the country's history. While the concept of a Westerner becoming a samurai may be problematic, it does highlight the ongoing dialogue between different cultures and the potential for new forms of identity and expression to emerge from this dialogue.

The Meiji period was a time of significant cultural exchange between Japan and the West. As historian and author Dr Donald Keene explains, *"The blending of different cultures is not always negative. The Meiji period was a time of significant cultural exchange between Japan and the West, and this exchange helped shape modern Japan into the country it is today."*

While the idea of a "western samurai" may be largely a work of fiction, the principles of Bushido, the samurai code of conduct, can still be relevant and valuable in modern society. The seven virtues of Bushido - rectitude, courage, benevolence, respect, honesty, honour, and loyalty - represent a set of values that can guide us in our daily lives and interactions with others.

Adopting the ways of the samurai does not mean adopting a rigid and outdated set of rules but rather taking inspiration from the principles and adapting them to our own lives and contexts. For example, practising courage and honesty can help us overcome challenges and build stronger relationships. Showing respect and benevolence towards others can foster a sense of community and mutual support.

However, it is important to note that not all aspects of samurai culture are applicable or desirable in modern society. For example, the strict hierarchical structure and emphasis on obedience to authority may not align with contemporary ideals of individual freedom and autonomy. Additionally, the samurai way of life was deeply rooted in violence and conflict, which is not necessarily compatible with a peaceful and just society.

Therefore, while the principles of Bushido can be valuable in guiding our personal behaviour and interactions with others, it is crucial to consider their context and limitations. Adopting the ways of the samurai should not mean blindly adhering to a set of rules or romanticising a bygone era, but rather taking inspiration from the virtues and adapting them to our own lives and values.

*The principles of Bushido represent a set of values that can guide us in our daily lives and interactions with others, even if we are not samurai.* According to Nitobe Inazo, author of Bushido: The Soul of Japan, *"While we may not be samurai, we can still learn from their code of conduct and apply it to our own lives."*

In conclusion, while the concept of a "western samurai" may be largely fictional, the principles of Bushido and the samurai code of conduct can still offer valuable lessons for modern society. By adapting the virtues of rectitude, courage, benevolence, respect, honesty, honour, and loyalty to our lives and contexts, we can cultivate a sense of personal and social responsibility that can benefit us and those around us.

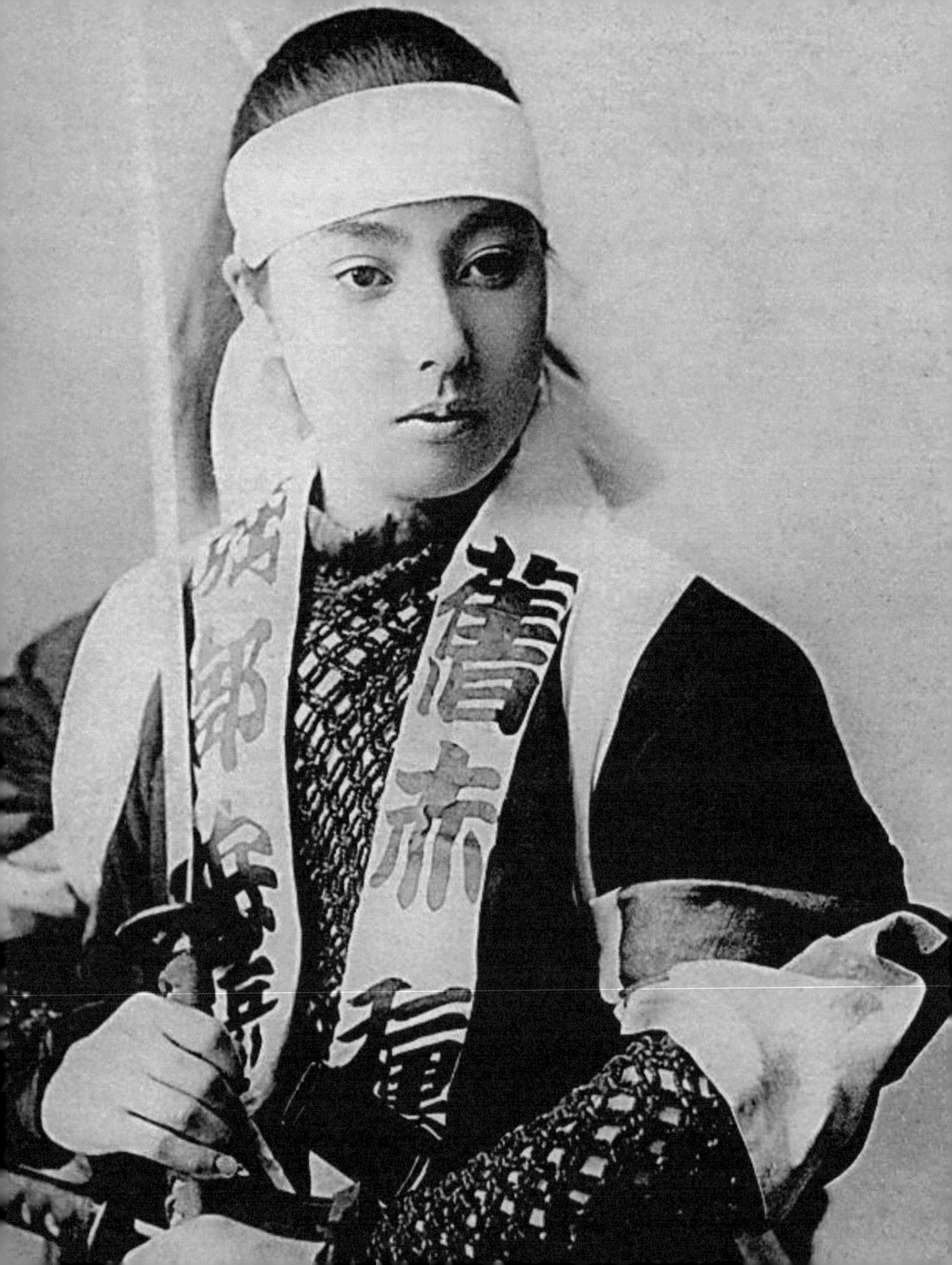

# THE SAMURAI WOMEN OF JAPAN

"The Onna-Bugeisha were women of remarkable strength, skill, and courage. Those who became samurai were held in the highest regard, not only for their martial prowess but also for their leadership abilities and dedication to duty. These women challenged gender norms and paved the way for future generations of women to assert themselves in traditionally male-dominated fields." - Kaoru Oka

In popular culture, the image of a samurai often conjures up a male warrior clad in armour and wielding his sword with deadly precision. However, the role of women samurai, or onna-bugeisha, is often overlooked. These skilled fighters were equally devoted to the samurai code of bushido and embodied the ideals of beauty, grace, and courage highly valued in feudal Japan. These women were not only fierce warriors but also cultural icons, representing the strength and resilience of women in a male-dominated society.

The *Three Great Onna-Bugeisha* refers to a group of legendary female warriors in Japanese history who have become iconic figures in Japanese folklore and popular culture. The great onna-bugeisha were Nakano Takeko, Tomoe Gozen, and Hangaku Gozen. These women were renowned for their exceptional martial arts skills and unwavering courage in battle. Their stories have been passed down through generations, inspiring countless works of literature, art, and media. Today, they continue to serve as symbols of the strength and determination of onna-bugeisha and the vital role of women in Japanese history.

Tomoe Gozen was one of the most famous onna-bugeisha. She was a skilled archer and swordswoman who fought for the Minamoto clan during the Genpei War in the late 12th century. According to legend, Tomoe was so beautiful and brave that she could defeat multiple opponents and emerge victorious. Her fellow warriors admired her bravery and skill; she is remembered as one of the greatest onna-bugeisha in Japanese history.

As Tomoe Gozen said, *'There is no shame in being weak; the shame is in staying weak.'*'

Another of the *Three Great Onna-Bugeisha* was Nakano Takeko, born in Edo (modern-day Tokyo) in 1847. She was trained in martial arts from a young age and became a skilled swordswoman. The Aizu domain recruited Nakano to fight in the Boshin War, a civil war fought between the forces of the Tokugawa shogunate and those seeking to restore the emperor's power. Nakano led a group of female warriors into battle, wearing a white kimono to signify that she would not surrender. She was eventually mortally wounded by a bullet, but before she died, she asked her sister to behead her and bury her head separately from her body so the enemy could not defile her corpse. Nakano's bravery and dedication to the samurai code of conduct continue to inspire people today.

Nakano Takeko famously said, *'I would rather be a caterpillar for a day than a butterfly for a lifetime.'* Her bravery and dedication to the samurai code were praised by Nitobe Inazo, who said, *'A sword is a weapon. Kenjutsu is the art of killing. Whatever pretty words you use to speak about it, this is its true nature. What Miss Nakano did was kenjutsu.'*

The onna-bugeisha were skilled fighters and played an important role in feudal Japan's cultural and political life. Women such as Tomoe Gozen, Nakano Takeko and Higuchi Kaneko were not just warriors but also scholars, poets, and artists. They were educated in the same subjects as men and often played important roles as advisors to their lords.

In addition to their martial skills, they were also expected to be knowledgeable about literature, history, and art and to embody the ideals of feminine grace and elegance.

The story of Higuchi Kaneko is celebrated in modern Japan. She was a prominent writer and political activist who advocated for women's rights during Japan's Meiji era. Despite coming from a low-ranking samurai family, she received a good education and became a teacher, which helped support her family. Her involvement in the Freedom and People's Rights Movement led her to become known as a feminist writer and speaker.

Kaneko was particularly active in promoting women's education, political participation, and economic independence. Her writings significantly impacted public opinion and contributed to the growing awareness and acceptance of women's rights in Japan.

In 1886, Kaneko became involved in the failed Hagi Rebellion, an attempt to establish a democratic state in Japan. She was charged with plotting to assassinate the emperor, and her involvement led to her arrest and sentencing to death. She was executed in 1896 at the age of 31.

Despite her short life, Kaneko's legacy as a feminist and political activist continues to inspire generations of Japanese women. Today, she is recognised as one of Japan's most influential advocates for women's rights, and her works are celebrated as an example of the strength and determination of onna-bugeisha throughout Japanese history

The onna-bugeisha were not the only women who fought in battles in feudal Japan. Some peasant women fought to defend their homes and families from invaders and bandits. These women, known as mura-musume, were often armed only with farm tools and had no formal training in martial arts. However, they were fiercely loyal to their communities and were willing to fight to the death to protect them. The mura-musume were not celebrated in the same way as the onna-bugeisha, but their courage and determination were just as admirable.

Despite their courage and skill, the onna-bugeisha were not immune to the constraints of gender roles in feudal Japan. They were expected to be wives and mothers first and warriors second, and their opportunities for advancement and recognition were limited. Nevertheless, many women samurai found ways to assert their independence and challenge traditional gender norms. They defied expectations by dressing in male clothing, speaking their minds, and refusing to be subservient to men. Their examples continue to inspire women today to challenge gender stereotypes and fight for equality and recognition in male-dominated fields.

The onna-bugeisha and mura-musume stories reveal women's remarkable resilience and courage throughout history, even in societies where they were typically oppressed or undervalued. These stories can inspire modern women, encouraging them to pursue their dreams and take on new challenges, regardless of societal norms or obstacles. By following the examples of these heroic historical figures, women can strive for greater equality and empowerment, paving the way for future generations.

Despite their many obstacles, the onna-bugeisha played an important role in Japanese society. Not only were they skilled warriors, but they also embodied the ideals of beauty, grace, and courage that were highly valued in feudal Japan. Their impact was felt in literature, art, and theatre, and they continue to captivate people to this day. Their image has become a powerful symbol of female strength and empowerment, inspiring women to break free from the constraints of societal expectations and pursue their ambitions.

Feudal Japan had several noteworthy female fighters, aside from the onna-bugeisha. Among them was Oichi, the sister of the renowned warlord Oda Nobunaga, who was celebrated for her political and military expertise. Despite being married to Azai Nagamasa, a rival of her brother's ally, the warlord Tokugawa Ieyasu, Oichi remained unwaveringly loyal to her brother and utilised her position to support his cause. She is remembered as a courageous and loyal woman whose contributions were significant during the turbulent politics of the Sengoku period.

Another female fighter was Mochizuki Chiyome, who is said to have trained a group of female ninjas, known as *kunoichi*, to infiltrate enemy territory and gather intelligence. Chiyome was the head of a ninja clan that warlords hired to carry out espionage and sabotage missions. She is remembered as a skilled and cunning warrior who used her femininity to her advantage.

The stories of these female warriors remind us that women have always been capable of incredible feats of strength and bravery, even in societies that sought to limit their opportunities and freedom. They defied gender norms and expectations, challenging the status quo and asserting their independence. Their examples inspire women today to pursue their passions and break through the barriers that stand in their way.

The onna-bugeisha and other female fighters of feudal Japan were remarkable women who defied gender stereotypes and fought for honour and glory alongside their male counterparts. They were skilled fighters, scholars, poets, and artists who played essential roles in Japanese society. Their stories remind us of women's strength and resilience throughout history and inspire women today who are seeking to challenge gender norms and achieve their full potential. The legacy of these women continues to inspire and empower women worldwide to push beyond the limitations that society has placed on them and strive for greatness.

Higuchi Kaneko was a prominent feminist and writer in Meiji period Japan. She was born in 1865 and became a pioneer of women's rights in Japan, advocating for women's education and equal rights. Higuchi Kaneko also wrote many novels and essays addressing topics such as gender inequality, women's education, and the role of women in society. She died at 24 due to tuberculosis, but her legacy continued to inspire many Japanese women in their fight for equal rights.

In a discussion on the power of choice, she stated that while *'life and death are in the hands of fate, we have the power to choose our own path.'* The onna-bugeisha and mura-musume demonstrated this by fighting for what they believed in, despite overwhelming odds.

As an anonymous author wrote, *'The courage of the onna-bugeisha and mura-musume should inspire us to never give up, even in the face of overwhelming odds. Their stories are the untold heroines of Japan's history.'*

陽　竹　健　白

竹　攢

睛明　　　　睛明

　　素
　　髎
迎香　　　　迎香

　　　　　　　　　　　和
　　　　人　　　髎
　　　　中

地倉　　　　地倉

# RONIN DOCTORS, SWORD DOCTORS AND HEALERS

Samurai doctors and healers played a crucial role in the health and well-being of their communities. They were skilled in the use of herbs and acupuncture and well-versed in the spiritual and mental aspects of healing. These individuals were highly respected for their knowledge and dedication to helping others, and their contributions continue to influence modern medical practices.

In feudal Japan, the samurai were the military nobility who served as the protectors and enforcers of their lords. They were highly skilled in the arts of war and were expected to be proficient in a wide range of martial arts disciplines. However, some samurai were also interested in medicine and became known as "ronin-doctors" or "sword doctors".

The term "ronin" refers to a samurai who has lost their lord or master, either through death or by falling out of favour. These samurai were often left without a means of support and would have to find other ways of making a living. Some turned to medicine and began practising as doctors, travelling from village to village and offering their services to the people.

The term "sword doctor" refers to the fact that these ronin-doctors were also skilled in using the sword and would sometimes use their martial arts training to help them in their medical practice. For example, they might use acupuncture needles to stimulate specific points on the body or use their knowledge of pressure points to help alleviate pain and discomfort.

While ronin-doctors were not trained as professional physicians, they did have a deep knowledge of traditional Japanese medicine. They were highly skilled in using natural remedies and techniques to treat various ailments. They were often called upon to treat injuries sustained in battle and more common illnesses and diseases.

Miyamoto Musashi is perhaps the most famous ronin-doctor in Japanese history, known not only for his legendary swordsmanship but also for his unique approach to medicine and bone-setting.

Musashi's medical knowledge was largely self-taught, and he developed his own system of healing that combined traditional Japanese medicine with his knowledge of martial arts. He believed the body was a self-healing organism and that the doctor facilitated the body's natural healing process rather than simply treating symptoms.

Musashi's bone-setting technique was particularly innovative. He used his knowledge of anatomy and martial arts to manipulate the bones and joints of the body, using pressure and leverage to realign them and promote healing. His techniques were known for being effective and relatively painless, and he was often able to heal injuries that other doctors had deemed untreatable.

In addition to his bone-setting skills, Musashi was also skilled in acupuncture and herbal medicine. He often used acupuncture needles to stimulate specific points in the body and promote healing. He would create custom herbal remedies to help treat a wide range of illnesses and conditions.

His Zen Buddhist philosophy profoundly influenced Musashi's approach to medicine. He believed that the mind and body were intimately connected and that a calm and focused mind was essential for healing. He encouraged his patients to meditate and practice mindfulness, often incorporating meditation and breathing exercises into his treatments.

While Musashi's medical practice was not without controversy, he was widely respected for his skill and knowledge, and he treated patients from all walks of life, from commoners to samurai lords. His legacy as a ronin-doctor has inspired generations of healers in Japan and worldwide, and his approach to medicine continues to be studied and practised today.

Yagyu Munenori was another renowned samurai who was known for his skills in both martial arts and medicine. As a member of the prestigious Yagyu clan, Munenori was trained in the art of swordsmanship from a young age, and he became an expert in the use of the longsword, the short sword, and the staff.

In addition to his martial arts training, Munenori was also deeply interested in medicine and healing. He studied the principles of traditional Japanese medicine and developed his own medical system that focused on using pressure points to alleviate pain and promote healing.

Munenori's system of pressure point therapy was based on the idea that the body contained a network of energy channels known as meridians and that by applying pressure to specific points on these channels, he could influence the flow of energy and promote healing. He believed that the body could heal itself and that by manipulating the energy flow through pressure points, he could facilitate the body's natural healing process.

Munenori's system of pressure point therapy was highly effective, and he was known for his ability to alleviate pain and treat a wide range of illnesses and conditions. He would often use his pressure point techniques in conjunction with herbal medicine and acupuncture to create a personalised treatment plan for each patient.

In addition to his medical skills, Munenori was also a highly respected teacher and philosopher. He wrote several influential books on martial arts and philosophy, including "The Book of Five Rings", which is still studied by martial artists and business leaders today.

Munenori's legacy as a samurai physician and philosopher continues to inspire people worldwide. His innovative approach to medicine and healing and his deep knowledge of martial arts and philosophy make him a true Renaissance man of Japanese history.

In addition to their medical knowledge, ronin-doctors were also skilled in the art of herbal medicine. They often used various plants and herbs to create natural remedies for their patients. They were known for their ability to diagnose and treat illnesses based on the patient's overall constitution and energy balance.

Despite their skill and knowledge, ronin-doctors were not always respected by the medical establishment of the time. Many traditional physicians viewed them as uneducated and uncouth, and their use of natural remedies and unconventional techniques was often criticised.

However, the ronin-doctors played an important role in the history of Japanese medicine, and their legacy can still be felt today. Many of the techniques and remedies they used are still practised in Japan. Their focus on natural healing and holistic medicine has influenced many modern approaches to health and wellness.

In conclusion, while the samurai were primarily trained as warriors, some were also interested in medicine and became known as "ronin-doctors" or "sword doctors". These skilled practitioners combined their knowledge of martial arts with traditional Japanese medicine, using natural remedies and unconventional techniques to treat a wide range of ailments. Despite being sometimes criticised by the medical establishment of their time, the ronin-doctors played a vital role in the development of Japanese medicine, and their legacy can still be felt today.

"Samurai healers were among the most respected professionals in Japanese society, and their role was as much spiritual and emotional as physical. They were expected to understand the importance of balance in the body and the need to take care of mental and spiritual health as well as physical health"

*Stephen Turnbull - The Samurai: A Military History*

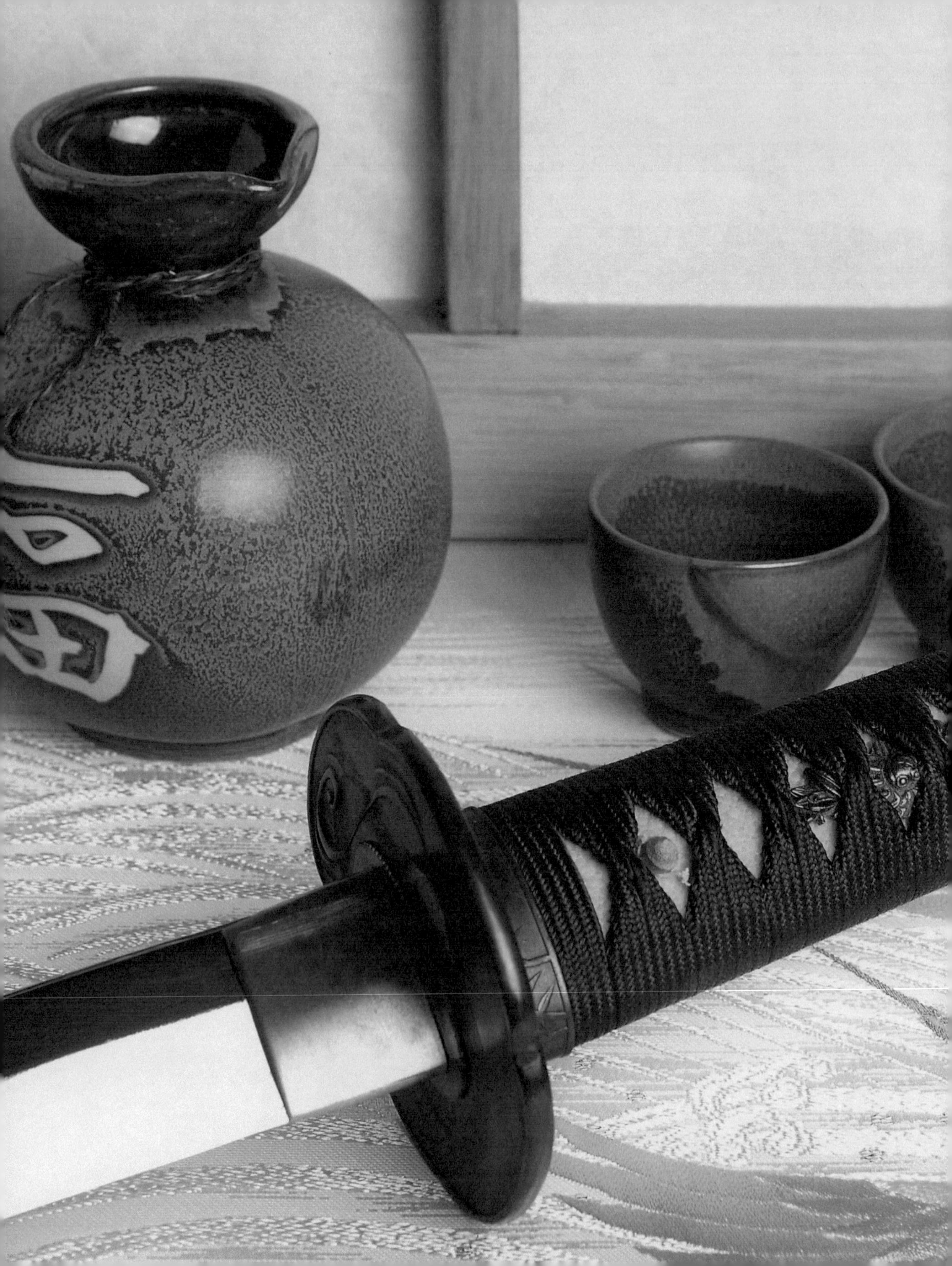

# ORIGINS OF THE BUSHIDO CODE

**Bushido derives from two Japanese characters: bu, warrior, and shido,** *way* **or** *path***. As a spiritual path, Bushido guided the samurai towards the pursuit of excellence in all aspects of life, whether in combat, art, or relationships and instilled a deep respect for the interconnectedness of all things.**

The Bushido code, also known as the way of the warrior, was the code of conduct and the moral principles that governed the behaviour of samurai warriors in feudal Japan. It was a complex and multifaceted system of ethics that emphasised a combination of martial and cultural virtues, including loyalty, honour, courage, self-discipline, and self-sacrifice.

The origins of the Bushido code can be traced back to the emergence of the samurai class in Japan during the 8th century. During this time, Japan was a collection of independent states ruled by local lords, known as daimyos, who maintained their own armies of warriors to protect their territories. These warriors, who were known as samurai, were often trained in the art of combat and were expected to be loyal and obedient to their lords.

Over time, the samurai developed their own unique code of conduct that emphasised loyalty, duty, and honour. This code was heavily influenced by the teachings of Confucianism, which emphasised the importance of hierarchy, duty, and respect for authority. In addition, the samurai were also heavily influenced by Zen Buddhism, which highlighted the importance of discipline, self-control, and the pursuit of enlightenment.

During the Edo period (1603-1868), the Bushido code became more formalised and codified. This was partly due to the efforts of powerful daimyos who sought to strengthen their authority and control over their samurai retainers. They did this by promoting the values of loyalty, honour, and self-discipline and encouraging their samurai to follow a strict code of conduct.

One of the most influential works on the Bushido code was the Hagakure, a book written by the samurai Yamamoto Tsunetomo in the early 18th century. The Hagakure was a collection of sayings and anecdotes that offered practical advice on living and dying as a samurai. It emphasised the importance of loyalty, honour, and self-discipline and provided a blueprint for the ideal samurai warrior.

The Hagakure is considered one of the essential works of the Bushido code, providing a wealth of insight into the beliefs and values of the samurai class. Some of the most famous quotes from the Hagakure include:

"On the battlefield, if you are not courageous, you will be killed. If you are not brave in other areas of your life, you will never be truly happy."

This quote emphasises the importance of courage and bravery in all aspects of a samurai's life, not just on the battlefield. It suggests that one cannot live a fulfilling life without these virtues.

"Accept everything just the way it is. Do not seek pleasure for its own sake. Do not, under any circumstances, depend on a partial feeling. Think lightly of yourself and deeply of the world."

This quote encourages samurai to embrace life's impermanence and avoid becoming attached to material possessions or personal desires. It also emphasises the importance of humility and the samurai's duty to serve the greater good.

"It is a good viewpoint to see the world as a dream. When you have something like a nightmare, you will wake up and tell yourself that it was only a dream. It is said that the world we live in is not a bit different from this."

This quote suggests that the samurai should view the world with a detached perspective, recognising that the physical world is impermanent and illusory. It encourages the samurai to focus on their inner character and values rather than external circumstances.

"Even if it seems certain that you will lose, retaliate. Neither wisdom nor technique has a place in this. A real man does not think of victory or defeat. He plunges recklessly towards an irrational death. By doing this, you will awaken from your dreams."

This quote suggests that the samurai should never give up, even when the odds seem insurmountable. It encourages the samurai to act with courage and determination, regardless of the outcome.

Overall, the Hagakure offers a comprehensive guide to the Bushido code, emphasising the importance of loyalty, honour, courage, and self-discipline. It remains an influential text to this day, providing valuable insights into the mindset and values of the samurai class

Another influential work on the Bushido code was the Bushido Shoshinshu, a book written by the samurai Taira Shigesuke in the mid-18th century. The Bushido Shoshinshu provided a more systematic and comprehensive overview of the Bushido code, outlining the virtues and obligations of the samurai warrior in great detail.

The Bushido Shoshinshu, which translates to "The Code of the Samurai," built upon the foundation laid by the Hagakure and expanded on the virtues and obligations of the samurai warrior in even greater detail. The book outlined eight virtues that were essential to the Bushido code: Rectitude, Courage, Benevolence, Respect, Honesty,

Honour, Loyalty, and Self-Control. These virtues were explored in depth, with examples of how they should be embodied in a samurai's daily life.

For instance, in the Bushido Shoshinshu, the virtue of Rectitude, or righteousness, was described as the essential quality a samurai could possess. Taira Shigesuke wrote, "The way of the samurai is found in death. When it comes to either/or, there is only the quick choice of death. It is not particularly difficult. Be determined and advance." This quote highlights the samurai's unwavering commitment to doing what is right, even at the cost of their own life.

Similarly, the virtue of Loyalty was emphasised as a fundamental aspect of the Bushido code. According to the Bushido Shoshinshu, "When one has said that he will perform a certain task, it is his duty to accomplish it, even if it means sacrificing his life." This quote illustrates the samurai's obligation to remain faithful to their lord and their duty, no matter the cost.

The Bushido code was also heavily influenced by the writings of Confucian scholars, such as Yamaga Soko and Arai Hakuseki, who emphasised the importance of loyalty, duty, and social order. These scholars argued that the samurai had an obligation to serve their lords and to maintain social harmony, even at the expense of their own lives.

Yamaga Soko, a prominent Confucian scholar during the Edo period, wrote extensively on the duties and obligations of the samurai class. In his work, "The Way of the Samurai," he stressed the importance of loyalty and self-discipline, stating that "the way of the samurai lies in loyalty and self-discipline. To serve one's lord with loyalty, to devote oneself to self-discipline, and to seek a true understanding of the world are the samurai's highest virtues."

Similarly, Arai Hakuseki, another influential Confucian scholar, believed that the samurai was responsible for maintaining social order and stability. In his work, "The Life of an Amorous Man," he wrote that "the samurai should not only serve his lord with loyalty but also consider the welfare of the people under his lord's rule. To be mindful of the common good is the ultimate duty of the samurai."

These ideas were incorporated into the Bushido code, which emphasised the samurai's duty to serve their lord and maintain social order, even at the cost of their own lives. The Bushido code was a complex and multi-faceted set of values and beliefs that influenced every aspect of samurai life, from their behaviour in battle to their conduct in everyday situations.

In addition to these influences, Japan's cultural and artistic traditions also shaped the Bushido code. The samurai were deeply involved in the practice of martial arts, such as kenjitsu and iaido, which emphasised discipline, self-control, and the pursuit of perfection. They also profoundly appreciated traditional arts such as calligraphy, poetry, and tea ceremony, which were seen as ways of cultivating refinement, self-discipline, and aesthetic sensibility.

The practice of martial arts and traditional arts in Japan played a significant role in shaping the values and principles of the Bushido code. The samurai's training in martial arts, such as kendo and iaido, emphasised the importance of discipline, self-control, and the pursuit of perfection. These skills were essential for battle, personal development, and spiritual growth. By mastering their chosen martial art techniques, samurai could cultivate the mental and physical discipline necessary to embody the ideals of the Bushido code.

Similarly, traditional arts like calligraphy, poetry, and tea ceremony were essential to cultivating refinement, self-discipline, and aesthetic sensibility. These arts required patience, attention to detail, and a deep appreciation of beauty and harmony. By practising these arts, samurai could develop the same qualities prized in their conduct as warriors, such as grace under pressure, a sense of proportion and balance, and an ability to appreciate life's fleeting and ephemeral aspects.

The Bushido and Western European chivalry codes are often compared, as they both emphasise virtues such as honour, courage, loyalty, and martial skill. However, while the codes of Bushido and chivalry share some similarities, they also developed in distinct cultural contexts and reflected different social, political, and religious beliefs. It is crucial to explore these differences in order to gain a deeper understanding of each code.

As we have seen, the code of Bushido emerged in Japan during a period of political instability and civil war known as the Sengoku period. During this time, the samurai emerged as a dominant class, serving as personal guards and administrators for local rulers. The samurai were expected to be skilled in the art of warfare and to demonstrate loyalty and obedience to their lord. Bushido emphasised the importance of the samurai's relationship with their lord and the value of sacrifice for the greater good. The code also placed great importance on self-discipline and stoicism, encouraging samurai to endure pain and suffering without complaint.

In contrast, chivalry emerged in Western Europe during the medieval period and was closely tied to the Christian faith. The code of chivalry emphasised the virtues of Christian piety, humility, and mercy. Knights were expected to be courageous in battle and show compassion and mercy to their enemies. Chivalry placed great importance on honour and the concept of the knight as a defender of the weak and vulnerable. Knights were expected to be generous and charitable and to uphold their lord's and faith's values.

One significant difference between Bushido and chivalry is the role of religion in each code. While Bushido was not explicitly tied to any particular religion, it was influenced by Japan's religious and philosophical traditions, including Confucianism, Buddhism, and Shintoism. These traditions emphasised the importance of honour, duty, and self-discipline, which were incorporated into the code of Bushido. On the other hand, chivalry was closely tied to the Christian faith, and many of the virtues emphasised in the code, such as humility and mercy, were rooted in Christian teachings.

Another critical difference between Bushido and chivalry is the social context in which each code developed. The samurai class in Japan was characterised by a strict hierarchy and social stratification, with the samurai at the top of the social order. This hierarchy was based on a system of feudal obligation, in which samurai were expected to serve their lord and uphold their honour. Chivalry, on the other hand, emerged in a more fluid social context in Western Europe, with knights often owing allegiance to multiple lords and kingdoms. This allowed for greater mobility and flexibility within the knightly class.

Finally, it is worth noting the different spiritual aspects of each code. While Bushido emphasised the value of self-discipline and stoicism, chivalry placed greater emphasis on the emotional and spiritual aspects of knighthood. Knights were expected to be loyal and chivalrous and demonstrate compassion and empathy towards others. This was reflected in the literature and art of the period, which often depicted knights as noble and virtuous figures, embodying the highest ideals of Christian chivalry.

While the codes of Bushido and chivalry share some similarities, they also reflect distinct cultural contexts and reflect different social, political, and religious beliefs. Bushido emphasised the importance of the samurai's relationship with their lord and the value of sacrifice for the greater good. In contrast, chivalry emphasised the virtues of Christian piety, humility, and mercy. Understanding these differences can provide insight into the values and ideals that shaped these two important codes of honour.

In conclusion, the Bushido code was the code of conduct and the moral principles that governed the behaviour of samurai warriors in feudal Japan. It was a complex and multifaceted system of ethics that emphasised a combination of martial and cultural virtues, including loyalty, honour, courage, self-discipline, and self-sacrifice. The origins of the Bushido code can be traced back to the emergence of the samurai class in Japan during the 8th century. During the Edo period, the Bushido code became more formalised and codified.

As I have described, the Hagakure and the Bushido Shoshinshu are considered to be two of the most influential works on the Bushido code. The Hagakure offers a comprehensive guide to the Bushido code, emphasising the importance of loyalty, honour, courage, and self-discipline. On the other hand, the Bushido Shoshinshu provided a more systematic and comprehensive overview of the Bushido code, outlining the virtues and obligations of the samurai warrior in great detail.

Some have suggested that the Bushido code is a relatively late invention, dating from the late 19th or early 20th century. In my opinion, this is based on either a misunderstanding of the nature of a code of ethics and principles, which must be fluid and adaptable, or on a misreading of the history around its adoption by the Japanese government as an aid to modernisation and industrialisation.

While the concept of Bushido as a formal code of conduct may have been a modern invention, it is clear that it was entirely based on a set of existing values and principles that guided the samurai's behaviour in earlier centuries. The Hagakure and similar texts provide evidence of a moral code for the samurai that emphasises personal integrity, loyalty, and martial prowess. The popularisation of Bushido as a formal code of conduct can be seen as a response to Japan's modernisation and westernisation, as the Meiji government sought to promote a sense of national identity and pride among the Japanese people.

So while the formalisation of Bushido in the late 19th century was a significant development in the history of the samurai code, it was not a creation ex nihilo. Instead, it was a process of articulating and codifying existing beliefs and practices that had been a part of samurai culture for centuries.

The principles and practices that make up Bushido, such as loyalty, courage, self-discipline, and self-sacrifice, were already deeply ingrained in the samurai culture and way of life. These ideas were passed down through oral tradition, literature, and examples of past samurai and were integral to the samurai identity and ethos.

Japan generally accepts the Bushido code as a genuine expression of an ancient code rather than a modern invention or interpretation.

While there may be some debate among scholars and historians about the exact nature and origins of Bushido, the principles and practices of the code are widely recognised as having deep roots in Japanese culture and history. These principles and practices were not only embodied by the samurai class but were also influential in shaping broader Japanese society and culture.

One reason for this widespread acceptance is that the principles of Bushido are deeply embedded in the Japanese language, literature, and art. For example, concepts such as loyalty, filial piety, and respect are fundamental values in Japanese culture and can be traced back to the samurai code.

Additionally, the samurai's legacy and Bushido's influence can be seen in many aspects of contemporary Japanese society, from the emphasis on teamwork and loyalty in the workplace to the importance of etiquette and politeness in daily interactions.

Of course, as with any cultural tradition, there may be variations in interpretation and understanding of the Bushido code. However, the general acceptance of Bushido as a genuine expression of an ancient code reflects many Japanese people's deep respect and reverence for their cultural heritage and history.

Today, the concept of Bushido continues to inspire and influence modern Japanese society, promoting values such as loyalty, honour, and discipline that are relevant to everyday life.

In the next chapter, we will delve deeper into the Bushido code, breaking down each of the eight virtues outlined in the Bushido Shoshinshu: Rectitude, Courage, Benevolence, Respect, Honesty, Honour, Loyalty, and Self-Control. We will examine the meaning of each virtue, explore its significance in the context of the Bushido code, and provide examples of how each virtue was embodied in a samurai's daily life. Through this exploration, we hope to gain a deeper understanding of the Bushido code and its enduring legacy as a symbol of samurai honour and courage.

○此時昇紙ヲ千枝程究リゴキ草摺
ノチヘレ端リ上へ出シ帯ニハセル也
○印籠竜金着ハ太刀ノ裏敏ニ通ス
○根付ナシ○引肌ハ常ノ如シ
倶ニ犬皮ナシヨシトス○傳ノ刀堅
メノ輪ハチリツバリ打絡ャリ
○帯ハ付ハ皮ヲ幅一丁ワニ
トリテ長サ四寸二ツ可付

一步三奥

小身旗ハ極上ノ黒布ヲ用深色各好ミニ任ル

# THE EIGHT VIRTUES OF BUSHIDO

Each of the eight virtues of Bushido demands that the warrior give up some part of himself in service of a greater ideal. Each call for selflessness, discipline, and courage. They are not only the virtues of the warrior; they are the virtues of any person who would seek to live a good life." - Nitobe Inazo. Bushido: The Soul of Japan

The code of Bushido is the ethical code that governs the behaviour of samurai warriors in feudal Japan. This code was influenced by Confucianism, Zen Buddhism, and Shintoism and was passed down through generations of samurai families.

At its core, the code of Bushido emphasised loyalty, courage, self-discipline, and honour. These virtues were seen as essential to the samurai's role as protectors of their lord and their people. The code of Bushido was not a written code but a set of principles and values that were passed down through oral tradition and practice.

The variation in the number of virtues listed in different sources on Bushido results from differing interpretations and translations of the code. As Nitobe Inazo writes in his influential book "Bushido: The Soul of Japan," "In the development of the code, confusion was bound to arise, variations and contradictions to occur." This confusion and variation have resulted in some sources listing seven virtues while others include an eighth, wisdom.

One explanation for this variation in the virtues is the dynamic nature of Bushido, which evolved over time and was influenced by various cultural and historical factors. In his book "The Samurai and the Sacred," Andreas Quast notes that "the code of Bushido was not static but developed over time, influenced by Zen Buddhism and Confucianism, among other factors."

However, regardless of the exact number of virtues, what is important is the values and spirit that they represent. As Paul H. Crompton writes in "Samurai Wisdom: Lessons from Japan's Warrior Culture," "The virtues of Bushido represent a code of conduct that emphasises honour, integrity, and self-discipline in all areas of life."

Therefore, while there may be variation in the number of virtues listed, the essence of Bushido remains consistent as a code of conduct that emphasises personal and moral development.

The *Bushido Shoshinshu,* or Code of the Samurai, is a text on the philosophy of Bushido written in the 18th century by Taira Shigesuke. The eight virtues of Bushido listed in the "Bushido Shoshinshu" are:

### Gi (Rectitude)

"Rectitude is one's power to decide upon a course of conduct in accordance with reason, without wavering; to die when to die is right, to strike when to strike is right." - Bushido Shoshinshu

### Yu (Courage)

"Courage is the power of the mind to overcome fear. It is not simply being fearless, but rather the ability to face fear and still act for the right thing." - Bushido Shoshinshu

### Jin (Benevolence)

"The spirit of benevolence is the spirit of seeking to promote the welfare of others. It manifests itself in the spirit of sympathy, charity, and forgiveness." - Bushido Shoshinshu

### Rei (Respect)

"Respect is the way of valuing people. When one recognises the dignity of others, he or she cultivates reverence, and thereby elevates his or her own humanity." - Bushido Shoshinshu

### Makoto (Honesty)

"Honesty is the root of Bushido. It is the principle that a samurai must follow at all times. By being honest, one can be trusted, and trust is the foundation of all human relationships." - Bushido Shoshinshu

### Meiyo (Honour)

"Honour is the driving force behind the samurai's actions. It is the source of his power and the foundation of his reputation. A samurai's honour is more important than his life." - Bushido Shoshinshu

### Chugi (Loyalty)

"Loyalty is the cornerstone of Bushido. It is the virtue that binds all the other virtues together. A samurai must be loyal to his lord, his family, and his friends. He must be willing to sacrifice himself for their sake." - Bushido Shoshinshu

### Jisei (Self-Control)

"Self-control is the foundation of the samurai's character. Without it, he cannot possess any of the other virtues. A samurai must have complete mastery over himself, his emotions, and his desires. Only then can he act with clarity and purpose." - Bushido Shoshinshu

The virtues of Bushido have had a profound impact on Japanese culture and continue to influence modern society. The eight virtues listed in the "Bushido Shoshinshu" offer a code of conduct for the samurai warrior, emphasising the importance of living a life of integrity, courage, compassion, respect, honesty, honour, loyalty, and self-control.

Each virtue has a unique significance and contributes to the overall philosophy of Bushido, which places a high value on personal and societal responsibility. To fully appreciate the depth and meaning of each of these virtues, it is crucial to take a closer look at their individual characteristics and how they were embodied and expressed by the samurai themselves. Each of the eight virtues has a rich history and significance, shaped by the unique culture and experiences of the samurai class. Examining their philosophy and values, we can better understand how the samurai lived out these virtues.

Let's take a closer look at each of the eight virtues:

## GI – HONESTY AND JUSTICE

Gi, or honesty and justice, was one of the most important virtues in the code of Bushido. The samurai were always expected to act honestly and fairly, tell the truth, keep their promises, and be just in their dealings with others. This virtue was essential to the samurai's role as protectors of their lord and people.

One of the most famous examples of Gi in Japanese history is the story of the 47 Ronin. In 1701, a samurai lord, Lord Asano, was insulted by a high-ranking official named Kira. In a rage, Lord Asano drew his sword and attacked Kira but could only wound him before being subdued. As punishment, Lord Asano was ordered to commit seppuku, a form of ritual suicide.

After Lord Asano's death, his retainers, known as the Ronin, were left without a master. For over a year, they plotted their revenge against Kira, eventually succeeding in killing him. However, they knew their actions were illegal and would result in their deaths. Before turning themselves in, they wrote letters explaining their actions and apologising for breaking the law.

The story of the 47 Ronin is a powerful example of Gi in action. The Ronin acted with honesty and fairness, seeking revenge for their lord's honour and accepting the consequences of their actions. They upheld their duty to their lord, even in the face of adversity and certain death.

Another example of Gi in Japanese history is the story of Oishi Yoshio, one of the leaders of the 47 Ronin. After the revenge was completed, Oishi turned himself in and was taken into custody. While in custody, he acted like he had gone insane, rolling around in the mud and drinking heavily. His captors believed that he had lost his mind and lowered their guard around him.

However, Oishi was simply biding his time. When the opportunity presented itself, he revealed his true self and committed seppuku, fulfilling his duty to his lord and his own sense of honour.

The story of Oishi Yoshio is a powerful example of the importance of deception and strategy in the samurai's code of Gi. Oishi acted with honesty, justice, and a keen sense of strategy, using deception to achieve his goal.

In addition to these historical examples, the samurai also had many sayings and teachings that emphasised the importance of Gi. For example, one saying goes, "It is the samurai's way to act with Gi, to be honest, and fair in all dealings, to be courteous and respectful, and to show courage in the face of danger."

Another teaching emphasised the importance of always speaking the truth, even if it is painful or difficult. The samurai were always taught to tell the truth, even if it meant admitting to a mistake or wrongdoing.

Another example of Gi in Japanese culture is the tea ceremony, which emphasises honesty and sincerity in all aspects of the ceremony. The tea master was expected to be honest in his intentions and actions and treat his guests respectfully and kindly. This emphasis on honesty and fairness was seen as essential to creating a peaceful and harmonious atmosphere during the ceremony.

Overall, Gi was one of the most important virtues in the code of Bushido, and it played a crucial role in shaping the samurai's way of life. This virtue was about honesty and fairness in dealing with others and living with a sense of honour and duty, even in the face of adversity and death.

The samurai's commitment to Gi was rooted in their role as protectors of their lord and their people. They were entrusted with the responsibility of maintaining order and justice in society, and they took this duty very seriously. To them, acting with honesty and justice was not just a matter of personal integrity but a way of upholding their commitment to their lord and their people.

The story of the 47 Ronin is a powerful illustration of the samurai's commitment to Gi. The Ronin's actions were about seeking revenge for their lord's honour and upholding society's principles of justice and fairness. By accepting the consequences of their actions, they demonstrated their willingness to live and die through their sense of duty and honour.

Similarly, the story of Oishi Yoshio demonstrates the importance of strategy and deception in the samurai's code of Gi. The samurai were expected to act honestly and fairly and use their intelligence and strategic thinking to achieve their goals.

The teachings and sayings of the samurai also emphasise the importance of Gi in their way of life. The samurai were always taught to act honestly and fairly, speak the truth even in difficult situations, and show courage in the face of danger. These teachings were not just abstract concepts but practical guidelines for living a life of honour and integrity.

In conclusion, Gi was a central virtue in the samurai's code of Bushido and played a crucial role in shaping their way of life.

## YU - COURAGE

Courage, or Yu, was the cornerstone of the samurai's identity. The samurai were expected to face danger and death without hesitation and protect their lord and people at all costs. This virtue was essential to the samurai's role as protectors of their lord and people.

One of the most famous examples of Yu in Japanese history is the Battle of Sekigahara in 1600. This was a decisive battle between two powerful factions vying for control of Japan. One of the Western army leaders, Ishida Mitsunari, called on his samurai to show courage in the face of overwhelming odds. Despite being outnumbered, the samurai charged into battle, showing incredible bravery and skill. The Western army was eventually defeated, but the samurai's courage and honour were remembered for generations.

Another example of Yu in Japanese culture is the story of the 47 Ronin, which I mentioned in the previous section on Gi. After their lord was forced to commit seppuku, the Ronin plotted their revenge against the man responsible. Despite knowing their actions would result in their own deaths, they showed incredible courage and determination in carrying out their plan.

In addition to these historical examples, the samurai also had many teachings and sayings that emphasised the importance of courage. For example, one saying goes, "The brave man is not he who does not feel afraid, but he who conquers that fear." This teaches that even the most courageous person will feel fear, but true courage lies in facing and overcoming that fear.

Another teaching emphasised the importance of mental and physical preparation. The samurai were trained to be prepared for any situation, whether it was a battle or a personal challenge. They were taught to develop the mental and physical strength necessary to face whatever challenges came their way.

The samurai also believed that true courage came from a sense of duty and responsibility. They saw themselves as protectors of their lord and their people and were willing to face any danger or hardship to fulfil that role. From a young age, this sense of duty and responsibility was ingrained in the samurai and was considered a crucial part of their identity.

Overall, Yu was seen as one of the most important virtues in the samurai's code of Bushido. The samurai were expected to show courage in all aspects of their lives, whether in battle or personal challenges. They were trained to develop the mental and physical strength necessary to face any situation and always act in their lord's and their people's best interests. This sense of duty and responsibility, combined with their courage and determination, made the samurai one of the most respected and revered classes in Japanese history.

## JIN – BENEVOLENCE AND COMPASSION

Jin, or compassion, was an essential virtue in the samurai code of Bushido. While the samurai were renowned for their martial prowess, it was understood that this strength needed to be tempered by kindness and empathy towards others. The samurai were expected to help those in need and to show compassion towards the less fortunate.

One example of Jin in Japanese history is the story of Tsunetomo Yamamoto, a samurai from the early 18th century. In his famous book, Hagakure, Yamamoto emphasises the importance of compassion towards others. He writes, "If a samurai has no compassion, he is no longer a samurai." Yamamoto believed that it was essential for the samurai to have compassion towards others, as it was a necessary counterbalance to their martial virtues.

Another example of Jin in samurai culture is the practice of Kintsugi or "golden joinery." This practice involves repairing broken pottery using lacquer mixed with gold or silver. Rather than trying to hide the damage, the repairs are made visible, creating a beautiful and unique piece of art. This practice is seen as a metaphor for the importance of compassion and empathy towards others. Just as the broken pottery is transformed into something beautiful, so too can people be transformed through acts of kindness and compassion.

The samurai also had many teachings and sayings that emphasised the importance of Jin. For example, one saying goes, "The purpose of the martial arts is not to conquer others, but to conquer the ego." This teaching emphasises that true strength comes from a sense of compassion and empathy towards others rather than a desire for power or domination.

The practice of Zen meditation was also an important aspect of Jin in samurai culture. The samurai cultivated a sense of inner peace and compassion towards others through meditation. Zen teachings emphasised the importance of letting go of ego and cultivating a sense of humility and kindness towards others.

Overall, Jin was seen as an essential part of the samurai's code of Bushido. It was not just a matter of personal virtue but also necessary for maintaining social harmony and order. The samurai were expected to show compassion towards others and to help those in need. This sense of empathy, kindness, and other virtues, such as honesty and courage, made the samurai one of Japanese history's most respected and revered classes.

In modern times, the value of Jin continues to be relevant. In a harsh and uncaring world, acts of kindness and compassion are more important than ever. By following the example of the samurai, we can cultivate a sense of empathy and compassion towards others and help to create a more peaceful and harmonious world.

## REI - RESPECT

Respect, or Rei, was one of the core values of samurai culture. It was a fundamental part of their identity and was deeply ingrained in their daily lives. The samurai were expected to show respect towards their superiors, peers, and inferiors, as well as the customs and traditions of their society.

In samurai culture, respect was a two-way street. Superiors were expected to treat their subordinates with respect and compassion, while subordinates were expected to show loyalty and obedience to their superiors. This mutual respect was essential to maintaining order and stability in society.

One of the most important forms of respect in samurai culture was respect for the sword. The sword was not just a weapon but a symbol of the samurai's identity and honour. Samurai were expected to treat their swords with the utmost care and respect and never to use them for anything other than their intended purpose.

Another important form of respect in samurai culture was respect for ancestors and tradition. The samurai believed their ancestors had paved the way for their success and that honouring their memory and upholding their legacy was their duty. They also thought that tradition provided a framework for their actions and decisions and that it was essential to respect and follow the customs and practices of their society.

Respect was also closely tied to the concept of honour in samurai culture. To the samurai, honour was not just a personal virtue but a reflection of their family and lord. By showing respect to others and upholding the customs and traditions of their society, the samurai believed they were maintaining their honour and the honour of those around them.

In conclusion, respect was a fundamental part of samurai culture. It was a two-way street, with superiors expected to show respect and compassion to their subordinates, and subordinates expected to show loyalty and obedience to their superiors. Respect for the sword, ancestors, and tradition was also important, as was respect for others and maintaining honour. By following these principles of respect, the samurai believed they were contributing to a stable and harmonious society.

## MAKOTO – SINCERITY AND HONESTY

Makoto, or sincerity, was a fundamental value underpinning the samurai code. The samurai were expected to be truthful, reliable, and straightforward in their dealings with others and to always act with integrity. This meant adhering to a strict moral code that placed a high value on honesty and sincerity and the ability to remain faithful to one's word, even in the face of adversity.

One of the most important examples of Makoto in Japanese history can be seen in the story of the 12th-century warrior Minamoto no Yoshitsune. Yoshitsune was a highly skilled and respected samurai who fought in the Genpei War between the Taira and Minamoto clans. He was renowned for his courage, martial prowess, and loyalty to his lord, Minamoto no Yoritomo.

However, despite his many accomplishments, Yoshitsune was eventually betrayed by his own brother, Minamoto no Yoritomo. Yoritomo feared that Yoshitsune's growing popularity and military strength threatened his authority, so he ordered his brother's capture and execution.

In the face of his brother's betrayal, Yoshitsune remained true to his principles of Makoto. Rather than flee or resort to violence, he accepted his fate and committed seppuku, the ritual suicide of the samurai. This act of self-sacrifice and loyalty has become a symbol of Makoto in Japanese culture. It is seen as an example of the samurai's commitment to living a life of honour and integrity.

Another example of Makoto can be seen in the practice of *ikebana* or Japanese flower arrangement. Ikebana is a highly refined art form that emphasises simplicity, elegance, and harmony and is based on the principles of Makoto. The arrangement of flowers is seen as a reflection of the natural world. As such, it is important to approach the art form with sincerity, humility, and deep respect for the natural beauty of the materials used.

In ikebana, the arrangement of flowers is not just an aesthetic pursuit but a spiritual one as well. It requires the artist to approach the materials with a sense of reverence and sincerity and to create an arrangement that expresses the beauty and harmony of the natural world. Through this process, the artist can cultivate a sense of inner peace and harmony and connect with the fundamental principles of Makoto that underpin samurai culture.

In conclusion, Makoto was a central value of the samurai code and was seen as an essential component of a life of honour, integrity, and self-discipline. Through examples such as the loyalty of Minamoto no Yoshitsune and the practice of ikebana, we can see how Makoto was expressed and embodied in Japanese culture and how it continues to influence our understanding of the samurai way today. As the 18th-century samurai scholar Yamamoto Tsunetomo once wrote, "In the way of the samurai, there is no greater virtue than Makoto."

The Samurai commitment to Makoto helped shape Japanese society and culture for centuries.

## MEIYO - HONOUR

Meiyo, or honour, was one of the most important virtues in the code of Bushido, the samurai's code of conduct. For the samurai, honour was more than just a personal attribute; it was a matter of moral responsibility, a duty to their family, clan, and lord. It was a quality that distinguished them from ordinary people and the foundation of their character.

*"The samurai has no money. He does not need money. He needs only his sword and his honour."* - Yamamoto Tsunetomo, author of Hagakure: The Book of the Samurai

Samurai were expected to uphold their honour at all times and to do nothing that would bring shame upon themselves, their family, or their lord. This was not just a matter of personal pride but a matter of obligation. To betray their honour was to betray their duty, loyalty, and identity as samurai.

The samurai believed their honour was bound up with the honour of their family, clan, and lord. If they lost their honour, they also lost the honour of those around them. The concept of honour was deeply ingrained in samurai culture and shaped every aspect of their lives. They followed the code of Bushido and upheld their honour, believing they were fulfilling their duty as warriors and human beings.

Seppuku, or ritual suicide, was considered an honourable way for a samurai to atone for a mistake or show loyalty to their lord. However, it was not the only way for a samurai to uphold their honour. The samurai also exchanged written oaths with their peers, promising to uphold their word and their honour. They engaged in duels to defend their honour, even if it meant risking their lives.

The samurai had strict rules about behaviour and etiquette designed to uphold their honour and dignity. They bowed deeply to their superiors, spoke formally and politely, and avoided any behaviour that could be seen as disrespectful or vulgar.

The story of Musashi Miyamoto, one of the most famous samurai in Japanese history, is often cited as an example of samurai honour. Miyamoto was not only a skilled swordsman but also a philosopher and strategist. His treatise on strategy, "The Book of Five Rings," is still studied by many today.

One of Miyamoto's most famous duels took place on the island of Ganryujima against Sasaki Kojiro, another renowned samurai. Miyamoto arrived late to the duel, purposely delaying his arrival to unsettle Kojiro. Despite the odds against him, Miyamoto emerged victorious with one stroke of his sword, using a technique called the "swallow's blade."

While some may question the tactics used by Miyamoto in this duel, it is vital to understand the cultural context in which it occurred. The samurai were not just skilled fighters but also strategists and tacticians. Miyamoto's delay and use of psychological warfare was a legitimate tactic in samurai culture. Additionally, the "swallow's blade" technique was highly skilled and precise, demonstrating Miyamoto's mastery of the sword.

But beyond his prowess in battle, Miyamoto also embodied the virtues of samurai honour. He believed in living a simple life, avoiding material possessions and excess. He also emphasised the importance of humility and self-improvement, stating, "From one thing, know ten thousand things."

Miyamoto's dedication to his craft and his moral code is a testament to the importance of honour in samurai culture. He lived by a strict code of conduct in battle and all aspects of his life. His example continues to inspire people worldwide to strive for excellence and live with honour and integrity.

Another example of samurai honour is the story of the samurai Kusunoki Masashige, who lived during the 14th century. Masashige was a loyal supporter of the emperor during the Nanboku-cho period, a time of civil war in Japan. He fought against the powerful Ashikaga clan, who had usurped the emperor's power and was eventually captured and executed. Masashige's loyalty to the emperor and his refusal to switch sides, even when it would have saved his life, has made him a symbol of samurai honour and loyalty.

Overall, honour was the most important virtue in the code of Bushido. It was a matter of moral responsibility, a duty to one's family, clan, and lord, and the foundation of the samurai's character. By upholding their honour, the samurai believed they were fulfilling their duty as warriors and human beings. The legacy of samurai honour continues to inspire people worldwide, reminding us of the importance of duty, loyalty, and moral responsibility.

## CHUGI - LOYALTY

Chugi, or loyalty, was a virtue of utmost importance in the code of Bushido, and it played a central role in samurai culture. The samurai were expected to be utterly devoted to their lord, to the extent of sacrificing their own lives for their master. Loyalty was considered a sacred obligation, and the samurai were trained from a young age to serve their lord with unquestioning devotion.

One of the most famous examples of samurai loyalty can be found in the story of Kusunoki Masashige. Kusunoki was a renowned samurai who fought for the emperor Go-Daigo during the Nanbokucho period, a time of civil war in Japan. When the shogunate forces defeated the emperor, Kusunoki continued to fight for his lord's cause, despite being vastly outnumbered and outmatched.

In 1336, Kusunoki led a force of only a few thousand men against a much larger army of the shogunate forces. Despite the odds, Kusunoki and his men fought valiantly, inflicting heavy casualties on the enemy. However, Kusunoki knew his forces were no match for the shogunate army and ordered his men to retreat. He stayed behind with a small group of his most loyal retainers, determined to hold off the enemy forces and buy time for his men to escape.

Kusunoki and his men fought to the death, refusing to surrender or retreat. Ultimately, they were all killed, but their sacrifice allowed many of Kusunoki's men to escape and continue the fight against the shogunate forces. Kusunoki's unwavering loyalty to his lord and commitment to the cause of the emperor became legendary, and he remains a symbol of samurai honour and devotion.

Another example of samurai loyalty can be found in the story of Honda Tadakatsu, one of the most famous samurai of the Sengoku period. Honda was a trusted general of the warlord Tokugawa Ieyasu, and he was known for his loyalty and bravery in battle.

During the Battle of Sekigahara in 1600, Honda led a force of 5000 men against a much larger army of the Western forces. Despite being vastly outnumbered, Honda and his men fought fiercely, inflicting heavy casualties on the enemy. Honda's helmet was knocked off during the battle, exposing his face to the enemy. Rather than retreating to put on a new helmet, Honda continued to fight without one, proclaiming, "A warrior does not need a helmet when he is born to be victorious."

Honda's unwavering loyalty to his lord and fearless courage in battle made him a legendary figure among the samurai. Even after his death, he continued to be revered as a symbol of samurai honour and devotion.

In addition to loyalty to their lord, samurai were also expected to be loyal to their fellow warriors. This loyalty, known as Giri, was based on the idea that samurai were part of a larger community that extended beyond their immediate lord. Samurai were expected to help and protect their comrades in arms, even if they were from a different clan or lord.

Overall, loyalty was a fundamental virtue in samurai culture and played a central role in shaping the samurai's identity. The samurai's unwavering devotion to their lord and comrades in arms was seen as a reflection of their honour and commitment to the ideals of Bushido. As the samurai Tokugawa Ieyasu once said, "The way of the samurai lies in absolute loyalty, obedience, and readiness to die for one's lord." This quote encapsulates the importance of loyalty in samurai culture.

Samurai loyalty was not just a matter of duty or obligation but also a matter of honour. For the samurai, honour was a concept that encompassed many virtues, including courage, loyalty, respect, and self-discipline. The samurai's commitment to their lord and comrades in arms reflected their honour and commitment to these virtues.

In addition to being loyal to their lord and comrades, samurai were also expected to be dedicated to their families. Family loyalty was a vital aspect of samurai culture and was considered just as important as loyalty to one's lord. The samurai were expected to defend and protect their families, even at the cost of their own lives.

One of the most famous examples of family loyalty in samurai culture is the story of Takeda Shingen, a powerful daimyo (feudal lord) during the Sengoku period. When

Takeda Shingen was attacked by his enemies, he ordered his family to flee to safety while he stayed behind to fight. Despite being severely wounded, he managed to hold off the enemy forces long enough for his family to escape.

Another example of family loyalty can be found in the story of Miyamoto Musashi, a legendary swordsman and samurai who lived during the 17th century. When Musashi's younger sister was threatened by a samurai from a rival clan, Musashi challenged the samurai to a duel and killed him. Musashi's willingness to risk his life to protect his sister is a testament to the importance of family loyalty in samurai culture.

Samurai loyalty was not limited to the battlefield. The samurai were expected to be loyal in all aspects of their lives, including their relationships with their superiors and subordinates. This loyalty extended to their duty as public servants, and the samurai were expected to serve their communities with dedication and integrity.

One example of samurai loyalty in public service can be found in the story of Honda Tadakatsu, a samurai who served under the Tokugawa shogunate. When Tadakatsu was appointed as the governor of a province, he made it his mission to improve the lives of the people in his jurisdiction. He worked tirelessly to develop infrastructure, build schools, and promote trade, all while maintaining a reputation for fairness and honesty.

In conclusion, loyalty was one of the most essential virtues in samurai culture. The samurai were expected to be loyal to their lord, their comrades in arms, their families, and their communities. Loyalty was not just a matter of duty or obligation but also a matter of honour and integrity. The samurai's commitment to their lord and their comrades were seen as a reflection of their honour and their dedication to the ideals of Bushido. As the samurai Tokugawa Ieyasu once said, "The way of the samurai lies in absolute loyalty, obedience, and readiness to die for one's lord." This statement perfectly encapsulates the importance of loyalty in samurai culture and its essential role in shaping the samurai's identity.

## JISEI – SELF-CONTROL

For the samurai, one virtue that stood out above all others was self-control or *Jisei* in Japanese. It was believed that a samurai who lacked self-control was a danger to himself and those around him, and could easily act dishonourably and bring shame upon himself and his lord.

Jisei was not just a matter of suppressing one's emotions or desires; it was a holistic approach to life that required one to be in control of their mind, body, and spirit. As the renowned samurai philosopher Yamamoto Tsunetomo wrote in his book Hagakure, "One who has mastered the way of self-control can never be controlled by others."

One example of the importance of self-control in samurai culture can be seen in the practice of *seppuku* or ritual suicide. Seppuku was considered a way for a samurai to regain his honour if he failed or acted dishonourably. However, seppuku could only be performed if the samurai had the necessary self-control to carry out the act with dignity and composure. As Yamamoto Tsunetomo wrote, "The essence of seppuku is self-control."

Another example of the importance of self-control can be seen in the tea ceremony or *chanoyu* practice. The tea ceremony was not just a way to enjoy a cup of tea but a way for samurai to practice self-control and discipline. The strict rules and procedures of the tea ceremony required the participants to remain calm and composed, even in the face of adversity or discomfort. As the 16th-century tea master Sen no Rikyu wrote, "The ultimate purpose of tea ceremony is not to drink tea but to cultivate a calm and peaceful mind."

Self-control was also crucial in the samurai's martial training. The samurai were trained to control their movements and actions, remain calm and composed in the heat of battle, and never lose focus or discipline. Without self-control, a samurai could quickly become reckless and endanger himself and his comrades.

One famous example of a samurai who embodied self-control was Miyamoto Musashi, a legendary swordsman who lived in the 17th century. Musashi was known for his mastery of the sword, but he also emphasised the importance of self-control in his teachings. He believed a true warrior should have complete control over his emotions and actions and that one could achieve greatness only through self-control.

In one famous anecdote, Musashi was challenged to a duel by a samurai who was known for his quick temper and lack of self-control. Musashi accepted the challenge but arrived at the duel several hours late, causing the other samurai to become increasingly agitated. When the duel finally began, Musashi could use his opponent's lack of self-control against him, ultimately defeating him with ease. As Musashi wrote, "The ultimate aim of martial arts is not having to use them."

Another example of the importance of self-control in samurai culture can be seen in the practice of iaido. This martial art emphasises drawing and cutting with the sword in a single fluid motion. Iaido requires tremendous discipline and self-control, as the practitioner must remain calm and focused even while performing a highly technical and potentially dangerous manoeuvre.

However, self-control was not just about mastering the body; it was also about cultivating a sense of inner peace and equanimity. As Yamamoto Tsunetomo wrote, "The true way of the samurai is not to fight but to be at peace with all things." This sense of inner peace was crucial for the samurai to maintain focus and composure in all aspects of their lives, from battle to daily interactions with others. It allowed them to approach even the most difficult situations with a clear and level-headed mind without being clouded by anger, fear, or other emotions that could lead to dishonourable behaviour.

One example of how the samurai's self-control extended beyond physical discipline and into the realm of emotional and mental control is found in the story of the legendary samurai, Yagyu Munenori. Munenori was a skilled swordsman and a renowned scholar and philosopher who emphasised the importance of inner calm and serenity in martial arts. He wrote, "The Way of the Samurai is the way of Zen. It is a way of acting without thinking, and thinking without acting."

Munenori's teachings focused on the idea that true self-control was not just about physical discipline but about the ability to control one's thoughts and emotions. He believed that by cultivating mental clarity and inner peace, the samurai could achieve a higher level of skill in martial arts and their daily lives.

Another example of the importance of self-control in the samurai's daily life can be seen in the practice of etiquette and proper behaviour. The samurai were expected to conduct themselves with dignity and grace, even in the most mundane situations. They were taught to remain calm and composed in all circumstances, whether dealing with a superior, a peer, or a subordinate.

One famous example of this emphasis on etiquette and proper behaviour is found in the book Hagakure, written by Yamamoto Tsunetomo in the early 18th century. As we have seen, the book is a collection of aphorisms and anecdotes that provide insights into the samurai's way of life. In one passage, Tsunetomo writes, "If one is not polite, then he is not a samurai. If a samurai has even a little disrespect, he is no longer a samurai."

This emphasis on proper behaviour and etiquette was not just a matter of social status or prestige but a fundamental part of being a samurai. By demonstrating respect and courtesy to others, even in the most mundane situations, the samurai maintained their sense of dignity and honour and upheld the values of Bushido.

In addition to etiquette and mental discipline, self-control was essential to the samurai's spiritual practice. Zen Buddhism profoundly influenced the samurai, emphasising mindfulness and self-awareness in all aspects of life. Through meditation and other spiritual practices, the samurai cultivated a deep sense of inner peace and clarity, which allowed them to remain focused and composed even in the most challenging situations.

One famous example of the role of spirituality in samurai culture is the story of Miyamoto Musashi. Musashi was not only a skilled swordsman but also a deeply spiritual individual who spent much of his life in pursuit of enlightenment. He believed that true mastery of the sword was not just a matter of physical skill but of spiritual discipline as well.

In his book "The Book of Five Rings," Musashi writes, "The Way of the warrior is the Way of the spirit." He believed that by cultivating a strong sense of spiritual discipline and self-control, the samurai could achieve a higher level of skill in martial arts and all other aspects of their lives.

The samurai believed in the concept of "enlightened warriorship," which meant that they were not simply fighting for personal gain or glory but for a higher purpose. This purpose was to serve their lord and uphold Bushido's values, including loyalty, courage, and selflessness. The samurai needed to cultivate inner peace and tranquillity to achieve this higher purpose. As Yamamoto Tsunetomo wrote, "The true way of the samurai is not to fight but to be at peace with all things." This sense of inner peace was crucial for the samurai, as it allowed them to remain calm and focused in the face of adversity and to maintain their honour and integrity in all situations.

In conclusion, self-control was essential for the samurai, encompassing physical discipline, mental and emotional control, proper behaviour and etiquette, and spiritual practice. By cultivating self-control in all aspects of their lives, the samurai could uphold the values of Bushido and become true warriors in every sense of the word.

As Miyamoto Musashi wrote, "The way of the warrior is like a mountain. It is steep, but those who climb it will find beauty in its view." The path of the samurai was indeed steep and challenging, but those who climbed it with dedication, discipline, and self-control found beauty and meaning in their lives and left a legacy of honour and nobility that still inspires us today.

## THE INVISIBLE NINTH VIRTUE OF BUSHIDO

### SELF-SACRIFICE

Self-sacrifice is often considered an implicit virtue in the Bushido code because it is closely tied to other virtues such as loyalty, honour, and courage. The Bushido code emphasises the importance of serving a higher purpose and sacrificing one's desires and interests for the greater good of society and one's lord or family. This willingness to sacrifice oneself for a greater cause is seen as an essential aspect of samurai ethos.

Moreover, the Bushido code is not a fixed set of rules but rather a collection of ideals that different samurai can interpret and apply in different ways in different situations. This flexibility allows virtues such as self-sacrifice to be emphasised or de-emphasised depending on the circumstances. Therefore, while self-sacrifice may not be explicitly listed as a virtue in the Bushido code, it is still considered an essential aspect of samurai culture and values.

Self-sacrifice was a common theme in samurai literature and poetry. One famous poem, attributed to the 17th-century samurai poet Matsuo Basho, reads:

*Winter solitude -*

*in a world of one colour*

*the sound of wind.*

The poem expresses the samurai's willingness to endure hardship and solitude for the sake of their duty and loyalty. It also conveys the idea of self-sacrifice to achieve inner peace and enlightenment.

Self-sacrifice was not just limited to the battlefield or acts of revenge or rebellion. It was also expected of the samurai in their everyday lives. For example, a samurai might sacrifice his own comfort or pleasure to fulfil his duty to his lord or family. He might also give up a position of power or wealth to serve a greater cause or live a more humble and honourable life.

The samurai's duty to their lord and their people was not just a matter of fulfilling obligations but of living according to a higher moral code. This code demanded that the samurai put the needs of others above their own desires and aspirations and be willing to make sacrifices for the greater good.

This attitude of selflessness and service was instilled in the samurai from a young age and was reinforced throughout their training and education. It became a way of life for the samurai, and they took it into every aspect of their lives. In this way, self-sacrifice was not just an abstract ideal but a concrete expression of the samurai's character and identity.

Another example of self-sacrifice in Japanese culture is the story of Oishi Chikara. Oishi was a samurai serving Lord Asano, the same lord whose death led to the story of the 47 Ronin. After Asano's death, Oishi and his fellow retainers became ronin and began to plan their revenge against the court official who had caused their lord's death.

However, Oishi realised that their mission was doomed to failure and that their actions would bring shame to their lord's name. Therefore, he devised a plan to mislead their enemies into thinking they had abandoned their mission. He spent two years living a life of debauchery and drunkenness to convince their enemies that they were no longer a threat. When the time was right, Oishi and his fellow retainers attacked their enemy's stronghold, successfully avenging their lord's death. Oishi's self-sacrifice, in which he put his personal feelings of vengeance aside to protect his lord's honour, exemplifies the samurai's dedication to their lord and their people.

Self-sacrifice was not limited to samurai culture alone but was a fundamental aspect of Japanese society as a whole. The concept of giri, or duty, was deeply ingrained in Japanese culture and demanded that individuals place the needs of their family, community, and country above their desires. This concept is still evident in modern Japanese society, where individuals are expected to work long hours and make personal sacrifices for their company or community's sake.

One example of this can be seen in the aftermath of the 2011 Tohoku earthquake and tsunami, which devastated large parts of north-eastern Japan. In the wake of the disaster, thousands of Japanese volunteers and workers risked their lives to help rescue those who were trapped or injured, despite the dangers posed by the continuing aftershocks and the threat of radiation from the Fukushima Daiichi nuclear disaster. These individuals demonstrated the same self-sacrifice and dedication to the greater good that was expected of the samurai in centuries past.

To conclude, self-sacrifice was a fundamental aspect of Japanese culture and society and was particularly emphasised in the code of Bushido that governed the samurai class. Whether on the battlefield, in acts of revenge or rebellion, or the everyday duties of life, the samurai were expected to place their lord's and their people's needs above their own personal desires. This concept of self-sacrifice remains an integral part of Japanese culture to this day and continues to inspire individuals to make personal sacrifices for the greater good.

右端列：平成十九年九月吉日建之　平成十八年三月吉日建之

京都市 株式会社 Rosnes 代表取締役 山口琢己
河野政子
大阪市東成区東中本 (有)山本範製作所
日下幸下戈ム 井上文雄
滋賀県今津町 (有)タチバナ
名古屋実業(株)
愛知県丹羽郡扶桑町高雄 清野貴祥 齋藤卓
東京 染谷裕之
新潟県上越市 田爪允 和子 由美子 享子
宮崎市 米喜工房
和歌山市島橋南ノ丁 津田産業(株) 津田幸也
愛知県高浜市 三洋グループ 神谷昭司
大阪市北区 田中ミナ子 小林塁矢子
福生教会 中山眼子
相和電気工業(株) 代表取締役 佐茂英四
株式会社エム・エー・シー 代表取締役社長 山口昭夫

# BECOMING AN EVERYDAY SAMURAI

Embodiment of the bushido code is not just a matter of memorising the eight virtues but a daily practice of living them in every aspect of our lives. By integrating these principles into our work, home life, relationships, and spiritual practice, we can cultivate a life of purpose, meaning, and excellence.

In the modern world, it's easy to feel disconnected from the past and the values that once guided our ancestors. However, we have seen how the essence of the bushido code, which the samurai of feudal Japan followed, still resonates with people around the world. The eight virtues of bushido: rectitude, courage, benevolence, respect, honesty, honour, loyalty, and self-control, have inspired many to live a life of purpose, meaning, and fulfilment.

Embodying the bushido code means living a life of integrity, where our thoughts, words, and actions are in alignment. When we embody the virtue of rectitude, we become grounded in reason and make decisions with clarity and purpose. This not only helps us in our professional lives but also in our personal lives, where we face difficult choices every day.

While the bushido code originates in feudal Japan, its principles are universally applicable in modern times. The virtues of bushido can help us navigate the complexities of the modern world and lead a more purposeful and fulfilling life. Whether we are facing challenges in our professional lives, personal relationships, or spiritual growth, the principles of bushido can offer us guidance and inspiration.

In the following chapters, we will explore applying these virtues to different areas of our lives, such as work, relationships, and personal growth. By cultivating these virtues, we can become more grounded, empathetic, trustworthy, and resilient individuals who inspire others to follow a path of honour and virtue.

Rectitude is the path of righteousness. It is truth and justice. When we embody the virtue of rectitude, we uphold a robust moral code and act with integrity in all aspects of our lives. This can lead to a sense of inner peace and confidence, where we know that we are living in accordance with our values. In the face of adversity or temptation, we stay true to our principles and make decisions based on what is right rather than what is easy. By practising rectitude, we become trustworthy and reliable individuals and inspire others to follow the same path of honour and virtue.

Courage is not the absence of fear but rather the ability to face it and act despite it. When we embody courage, we are empowered to step out of our comfort zones and confidently pursue our goals. This can be especially valuable in the workplace, where taking risks and standing up for what we believe in can lead to growth and success.

Benevolence is the spirit of seeking to promote the welfare of others. When we embody the virtue of benevolence, we become more empathetic and compassionate, and we strive to help others without expecting anything in return. This can lead to more meaningful relationships where we support each other and create a sense of community.

Respect is a way of valuing people. When we embody the virtue of respect, we cultivate reverence for ourselves and others. This leads to healthier relationships, where we communicate with kindness and empathy and treat others how we want to be treated.

Honesty is the root of bushido. When we embody the virtue of honesty, we become trustworthy and reliable. This can lead to stronger professional relationships, where our colleagues and clients know they can depend on us. It can also lead to deeper personal relationships where we are open and transparent with our loved ones.

Honour is the driving force behind the samurai's actions. When we embody the virtue of honour, we hold ourselves to a higher standard of conduct. This can lead to a sense of pride and accomplishment, where we know we are doing the right thing, even when it's difficult.

Loyalty is the cornerstone of bushido. When we embody the virtue of loyalty, we become committed to our families, friends, and colleagues. This can lead to stronger relationships, where we support each other through thick and thin and work together towards common goals.

Self-control is the foundation of the samurai's character. When we embody the virtue of self-control, we become masters of our emotions and desires. This can lead to more balanced and fulfilling lives where we make decisions based on reason rather than impulse.

By embodying the eight virtues of bushido, we can enhance every aspect of our lives. We can become more grounded, confident, empathetic, trustworthy, honourable, loyal, and self-controlled.

One of the critical aspects of bushido is the pursuit of excellence. This means striving for mastery in every aspect of our lives, whether it's our work, relationships, or personal growth. By committing ourselves to the pursuit of excellence, we can develop a sense of purpose and direction that drives us forward.

Another essential aspect of bushido is the cultivation of character. This means embodying traits such as honesty, integrity, and self-discipline in all areas of our lives. By developing a strong character, we can become more trustworthy and reliable individuals who are respected by others.

Bushido also emphasises the importance of harmony and balance. This means finding a sense of equilibrium between our physical, emotional, and spiritual selves. By achieving balance in our lives, we can cultivate a sense of inner peace and contentment that allows us to live more fully in the present moment.

Ultimately, the principles of bushido are about living a life of meaning and purpose. By embodying these principles, we can cultivate a sense of inner strength and resilience that enables us to overcome adversity and achieve our goals. Whether we are seeking success in our careers, fulfilment in our relationships, or personal growth and self-discovery, the principles of bushido offer a roadmap for living a virtuous and meaningful life

All I need from you is a desire to live your best life and step outside of the mundane and ordinary. You can be ordinary, of course. Everyone is ordinary. But you can be extraordinary, too, if you make that choice.

But the desire to live your best life is not enough on its own. It requires action, commitment, and perseverance. It requires a willingness to push beyond your limits and confront your fears. You must be willing to face the unknown and embrace uncertainty. This is where growth happens. This is where you will find your true potential.

The road to an extraordinary life is not easy. It will be filled with challenges, setbacks, and obstacles. But it is in these moments that you will discover your inner strength and resilience. You will learn to persevere and overcome adversity. You will develop a more profound sense of self-awareness and self-confidence.

To create a virtuous life, you must first identify what that means for you. What values do you hold dear? What kind of person do you want to be? What kind of life do you want to lead? Once you clearly understand your vision for your life, you can begin to take the steps necessary to make it a reality.

It may mean stepping out of your comfort zone and trying new things. It may mean taking risks and facing your fears. It may mean abandoning old habits and beliefs that no longer serve you. But in these moments of discomfort and uncertainty, you will find the strength and courage to create the life you truly desire.

Remember, everything you desire is on the other side of your comfort zone. The life you want to live is waiting for you. But it will not come to you without effort and discipline. You must be willing to put in the work and make the necessary sacrifices. You must be willing to persevere through the tough times and stay committed to your vision.

So, are you ready to step outside of the mundane and ordinary? Are you prepared to create a truly extraordinary life? The choice is yours. You have the power to create the life you want. All it takes is a desire to live your best life and the willingness to take action.

Once you have made the decision to step outside of your comfort zone and embark on the journey towards an extraordinary life, you will undoubtedly encounter obstacles and setbacks. It's important to remember that this is a natural part of the process, and how you respond to these challenges will ultimately determine your success.

Giving up or returning to your old ways can be tempting when faced with adversity. But it's during these difficult moments that you must draw upon your inner strength and perseverance. It's important to stay focused on your goals and remind yourself why you started this journey in the first place.

Along the way, you may also encounter criticism or naysayers who doubt your ability to succeed. Don't let their negativity discourage you. Remember that the path towards greatness is often lonely and requires a steadfast belief in yourself and your vision.

Finally, it's important to celebrate your victories along the way, no matter how small they may seem. Recognise and acknowledge your progress, and use it as fuel to keep pushing forward towards your goals.

Living an extraordinary life requires a willingness to step outside your comfort zone, a strong desire to grow and improve, and the perseverance to overcome obstacles and setbacks. But with these qualities, anything is possible. So what are you waiting for? Take the first step towards your best life today.

## STRATEGIES

In the following chapters, you will see the eight virtues of Bushido and various methods by which you can start the process of embodiment. There are accessible daily practices focused on home life, work, relationships and spirituality. There are mediations, both short and long, and there are affirmations. Taken together, they create a synthesis of practical techniques that can, over time, transform how your mind works, creating profound psychological and emotional shifts.

But what is the best way to start, and how can you most effectively move forward?

There is no single correct answer and no single most effective way. And that is the beauty of this process. You can explore it and make it your own. Intuitive practice s always the best approach. Let the activity and practice lead you, and don't stress. Don't judge yourself. Effectively, you must play at this process. Experiment as if you were a child. Enjoy the change. Enjoy any pushback and resistance too. It shows you are winning. Just treat it as fun.

The best approach is always in moderation and experimentation.

Don't do too much too soon. Start as you mean to go on. Please don't plan a daily routine that will take an hour or two hours every day, no matter how excited you may feel, as it is unlikely to be sustainable.

Better to start with ten minutes a day and gradually build it up over the weeks and months to come. Even ten minutes, done consistently and diligently, can create profound, life-changing shifts.

Let's look at an example:

Start with Rectitude. Perhaps choose one activity from each category and decide to focus on that for a week. So one activity to promote change in your home life, work life, relationships, and for your higher self. Perhaps also choose the short meditation, and perform it every day or several times a week. If you are feeling very motivated, choose some affirmations too. Memorise them, or write them down. You could start your day with five minutes of affirmations. Or chant them on your way to work or during any downtime during the day.

After a week has passed, you could look to the next virtue. Courage. And do the same again. You could also continue using the Rectitude affirmations to continue the process of embodying rectitude, while drawing in the quality of courage.

Allow the practice to grow and expand. Experiment with it, and allow it to teach you.

You could work your way through all eight of the virtues in order. Alternatively, you could think about the virtues you want to embody, or perhaps the ones you most need to embody and focus initially on those. It might be an idea to speak to close friends or family and discover which virtues they think you lack or need to strengthen. Be prepared to be offended and upset. You might not like what you hear.

We tend to train our strengths and ignore our weaknesses. It's natural. So our strengths become stronger, and our weaknesses become magnified. Athletes who can identify their weaknesses and train them become champions in sport. The rest of us train our strengths because it feels good, but we stall our progress in doing so.

So be honest with yourself.

Which virtues do you need to strengthen, and which virtues are already strong? Focus on the areas of weakness. Not the areas where you are already strong.

Be realistic about the time you have available. Don't plan to wake up an hour early to meditate if you know you'll be too tired to focus. Don't plan to try all the activities for work and home life if doing so will stress you and make you feel like you have failed.

Be kind to yourself.

Enjoy this process. It will take time. It can't be hurried, and it can't be bullied. Most of us, myself included, overestimate what we can achieve in a day and underestimate what we can achieve in a year.

Just ten minutes a day of steady and diligent work over the next twelve months will create enormous and profound changes beyond your wildest expectations.

Now is your chance to take action that your future self will thank you for.

There is nothing to stop you. You've got this.

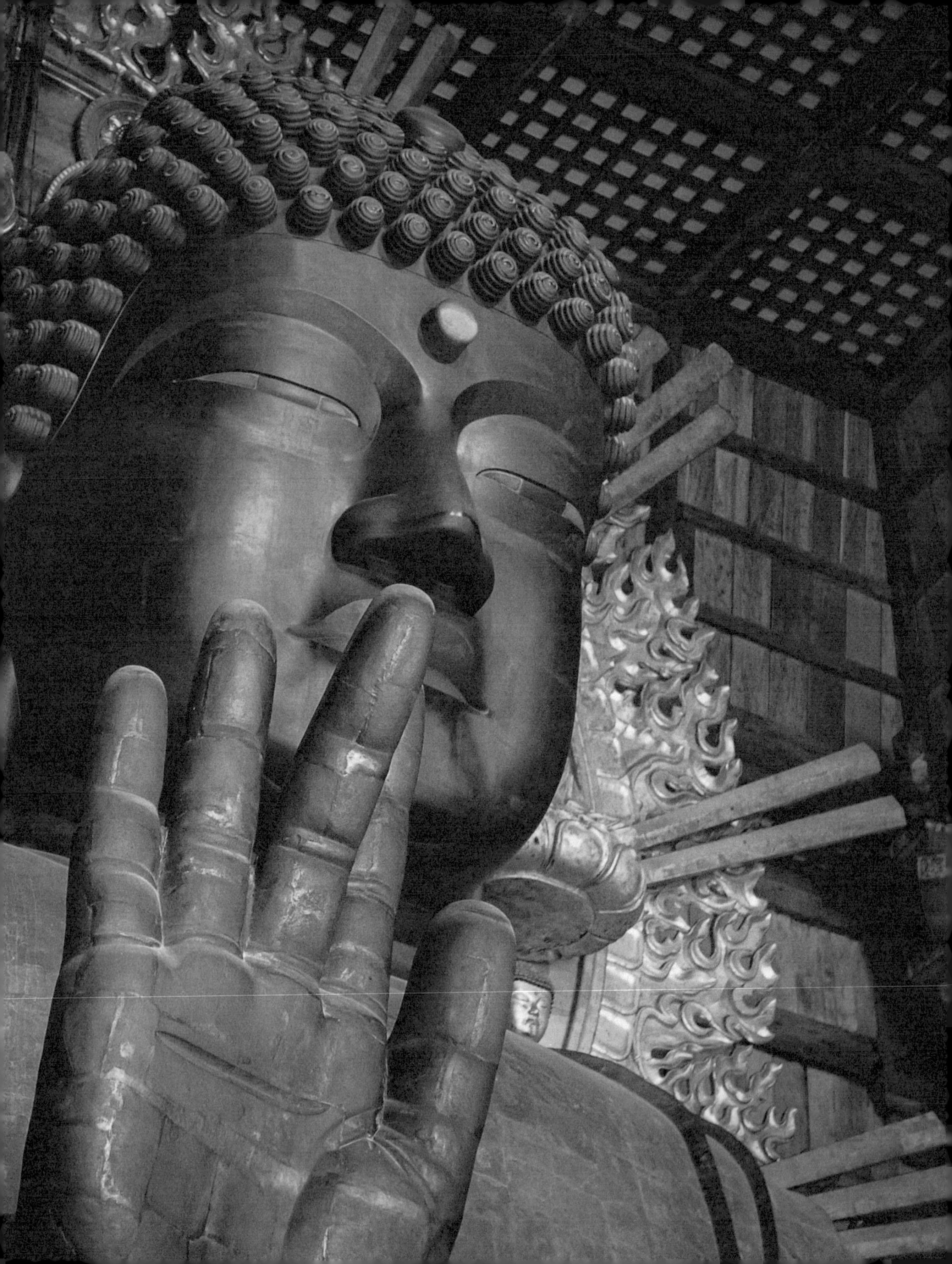

# RECTITUDE
## RIGHTEOUSNESS, TRUTH AND JUSTICE

"Cultivate the root of the tree of your mind so that it may grow into a garden of righteousness, making not a mistake even in dreams." - Tsunetomo Yamamoto.

This quote emphasises the importance of cultivating a mind that is rooted in righteousness and honesty, even to the point of being mindful of one's thoughts and dreams. It highlights the idea that genuine rectitude must be a constant practice, not just something that is exhibited in one's actions but also in one's thoughts and innermost being.

Achieving lasting change requires continuous and diligent effort. When we attempt to change old patterns, these patterns will resist and reassert themselves. Thus, we must persist in our efforts until we finally break the habit. Although the process is not easy, every day of trying brings us one step closer to success. As long as we keep trying, we cannot fail. With each passing day, the journey becomes easier.

Embodying rectitude, truth, and honesty in different areas of our lives requires conscious effort and daily practice. But these practices aren't complicated. They just need you to make an effort. They just require you to get out of bed and commit to change.

Here are some practices, meditations, and approaches to help you bring truth and honesty to four different arenas:

## At Home

Practice active listening: Listen to your family members without interrupting or judging them. Please give them your full attention and be empathetic.

Express your feelings: Be honest about your feelings and communicate them clearly and respectfully. Avoid passive-aggressive behaviour.

Keep your promises: If you promise to do something, make sure you follow through. This will build trust and respect within your family.

Apologise when you're wrong: Take responsibility for your mistakes and apologise sincerely.

Be truthful about your limitations: If you can't fulfil a request or task, be honest about it instead of over-committing.

Practice forgiveness: Let go of grudges and resentments and forgive others for their mistakes.

## At Work

Be transparent: Communicate openly and honestly with your colleagues and superiors. Don't hide mistakes or problems.

Admit when you're wrong: If you make a mistake, own up to it and take responsibility. This will build credibility and trust with your co-workers.

Avoid gossip: Refrain from spreading rumours or talking behind people's backs. Instead, address issues directly with those involved.

Speak up when you see something unethical: If you witness unethical behaviour or actions, speak up and report it to the appropriate channels.

Avoid conflicts of interest: Be transparent about any potential conflicts of interest and take steps to mitigate them.

Offer constructive feedback: Be honest and constructive when providing feedback to colleagues. Focus on the behaviour or actions, not the person.

## In Our Relationships

Be vulnerable: Share your thoughts and feelings with your partner. This will foster intimacy and trust.

Practice empathy: Try to see things from your partner's perspective and understand their feelings.

Be honest about your boundaries: Communicate your needs and boundaries clearly and respectfully.

Respect and honour others' boundaries: Be mindful of others' boundaries. Avoid pushing others to do something they're uncomfortable with.

Practice active compassion: Show kindness and compassion to others, even when they make mistakes or have different opinions.

Be accountable for your actions: If you hurt someone's feelings or cause harm, take accountability for your actions and work towards making amends.

## In a Spiritual Sense

Practice self-reflection: Take time to reflect on your actions and motivations. Are you living in alignment with your values?

Seek truth: Explore different perspectives and seek truth and knowledge in all aspects of your life.

Practice mindfulness: Cultivate awareness of your thoughts and actions. This will help you live in accordance with your values and maintain integrity.

Practice gratitude: Focus on what you're grateful for in your life, and express gratitude regularly.

Engage in self-care: Take care of yourself physically, mentally, and emotionally. This will help you live in alignment with your values and maintain integrity.

Seek feedback: Ask for feedback from trusted sources, and be open to constructive criticism. This will help you grow and develop in your personal and spiritual life.

Remember that embodying rectitude takes time and effort. Start small and be consistent in your practice. With time, you will see positive changes in your way of being and the lives of those around you.

## Meditations to Embody Rectitude

### Short meditation

#### 5-10 minutes daily

**A Breath of Truth meditation, in which you focus on your breath and breathe in the intention of truth and honesty, is a profound way to shift your ability to embody integrity and truth.**

Step 1: Find a quiet, comfortable place where you won't be disturbed for the duration of your meditation. Sit in a comfortable cross-legged position on the floor, on a cushion, or in a chair, with your back straight and your hands resting on your knees. You can also lie down.

Step 2: Close your eyes and take a few deep breaths, allowing your body to relax and your mind to become calm.

Step 3: Focus your attention on your breath, noticing the sensation of the air moving in and out of your body. Imagine that with each inhale, you're breathing in the intention of truth and honesty.

Step 4: As you inhale, visualise a bright light filling your body, representing the energy of truth and honesty. Allow this light to expand with each breath, filling your entire being.

Step 5: Hold your breath for a few moments, allowing the energy of truth and honesty to fill every cell of your body.

Step 6: As you exhale, imagine any untruths or dishonesties you may be holding onto, leaving your body with your breath.

Step 7: Repeat this process for several breaths, focusing on the intention of truth and honesty with each inhale and exhale.

Step 8: As you continue to breathe in the energy of truth and honesty, allow any thoughts or feelings that arise to pass through your mind without judgement or attachment simply. If you notice yourself getting distracted or caught up in a thought, gently bring your attention back to your breath and the intention of truth and honesty.

Step 9: Take a few moments to reflect on any areas of your life where you may not have been entirely truthful or honest. Allow yourself to feel any emotions that come up, and then visualise the bright light filling those areas with the energy of truth and honesty.

Step 10: When you're ready, take a deep breath in and slowly exhale. Take a moment to acknowledge the shift that has taken place within you, and then gently open your eyes.

Congratulations

You've completed a Breath of Truth meditation, which can be a powerful tool for cultivating a greater sense of integrity and authenticity in your life. Repeat this meditation as often as you like to reinforce your commitment to embodying truth and honesty.

## Long Meditation

*20-30 minutes daily or several times a week.*

**A Truth and Honesty meditation, in which you focus on being truthful and honest with yourself and others, is a powerful way to introduce yourself to deeper levels of truth, integrity and authenticity.**

Step 1: Find a quiet, comfortable place where you won't be disturbed for the duration of your meditation. Sit in a comfortable cross-legged position on the floor or on a cushion, or sit on a chair with your back straight and your hands resting on your knees.

Step 2: Close your eyes and take a few deep breaths, allowing your body to relax and your mind to become calm.

Step 3: Visualise a bright light surrounding you, representing truth and honesty. Imagine this light filling your entire body, from the top of your head down to the tips of your toes.

Step 4: Repeat the following affirmation to yourself, either silently or out loud: "I am committed to being truthful and honest with myself and others. I speak my truth with kindness and compassion, and I live my life with integrity."

Step 5: As you continue to focus on the bright light surrounding you, allow any thoughts or feelings that arise to pass through your mind without judgement or attachment simply. If you notice yourself getting distracted or caught up in a thought, gently bring your attention back to your breath and the bright light surrounding you.

Step 6: Take a few moments to reflect on any areas of your life where you may not have been completely honest with yourself or others. Allow yourself to feel any emotions that come up, and then visualise the bright light surrounding you, filling those areas with truth and honesty.

Step 7: When you're ready, take a deep breath in and slowly exhale. Take a moment to acknowledge your commitment to being truthful and honest, then gently open your eyes.

Congratulations.

You've completed a meditation focused on truth and honesty. Repeat this meditation as often as you like to reinforce your commitment to living a life filled with integrity and authenticity.

## Visualisation

**A short visualisation, practised at any time of the day, can be a powerful tool to shift your perspective.**

Imagine yourself standing in a bright white light, symbolising the purity of truth and honesty. Imagine this light filling you up and radiating out from you, representing your commitment to living a life of rectitude.

## Affirmations

**Choose a single affirmation you are attracted to or several affirmations, and write them down or memorise them. You can add them to notes around the house. Pin them where you can see them. Chant them to yourself. Sing them. Start the day with some affirmations. Affirmations are a proven way to programme your subconscious, creating profound change.**

I am a person of integrity, and I always do the right thing, even when it's difficult.

My words and actions are always in alignment with my values and beliefs.

I am honest with myself and others, and I speak my truth with compassion and kindness.

I trust myself to make decisions that are in alignment with my highest good and the highest good of others.

I am authentic and true to myself, and I allow others to do the same.

I am committed to living my life with integrity and making choices that align with my highest self.

I am worthy of love and respect, and I treat myself and others with kindness and compassion.

I am open and receptive to feedback that helps me grow and improve as a person.

I am willing to take responsibility for my actions and make amends when necessary.

I trust that the universe supports me in living a life of truth, integrity, and authenticity.

I always speak the truth with clarity and conviction, knowing that honesty is the foundation of trust and respect.

I honor my values and principles, and I stay true to myself even in the face of adversity or temptation.

My actions reflect my commitment to integrity and truth, and I am accountable for the impact I have on others.

I embrace my imperfections and strive to learn from my mistakes, knowing that self-awareness and self-reflection are key to personal growth and development.

I recognise that my words and actions have the power to create positive change in the world, and I use this power responsibly, with compassion and empathy for all beings.

Repeat these affirmations to yourself regularly, either silently or out loud, to help shift your mindset and cultivate a greater sense of rectitude, truth, integrity, and authenticity in your life.

Developing and embodying rectitude and justice in our lives is a lifelong process that requires dedication, self-reflection, and action. At its core, rectitude refers to a strong commitment to doing what is right, while justice involves treating all individuals fairly and impartially. By actively cultivating these virtues, we can create a more equitable and just world for ourselves and those around us.

The process of embodying rectitude and justice requires us to first examine our own beliefs and actions. We must be honest with ourselves about any biases or prejudices we may hold, and work to address and challenge them. This involves actively seeking out diverse perspectives and experiences, and being open to feedback and criticism. We must also strive to act in accordance with our values, even when it may be difficult or unpopular. By doing so, we can build a reputation for being trustworthy and just, and inspire others to do the same. Ultimately, embodying rectitude and justice is not just a personal goal, but a collective responsibility to create a better world for all

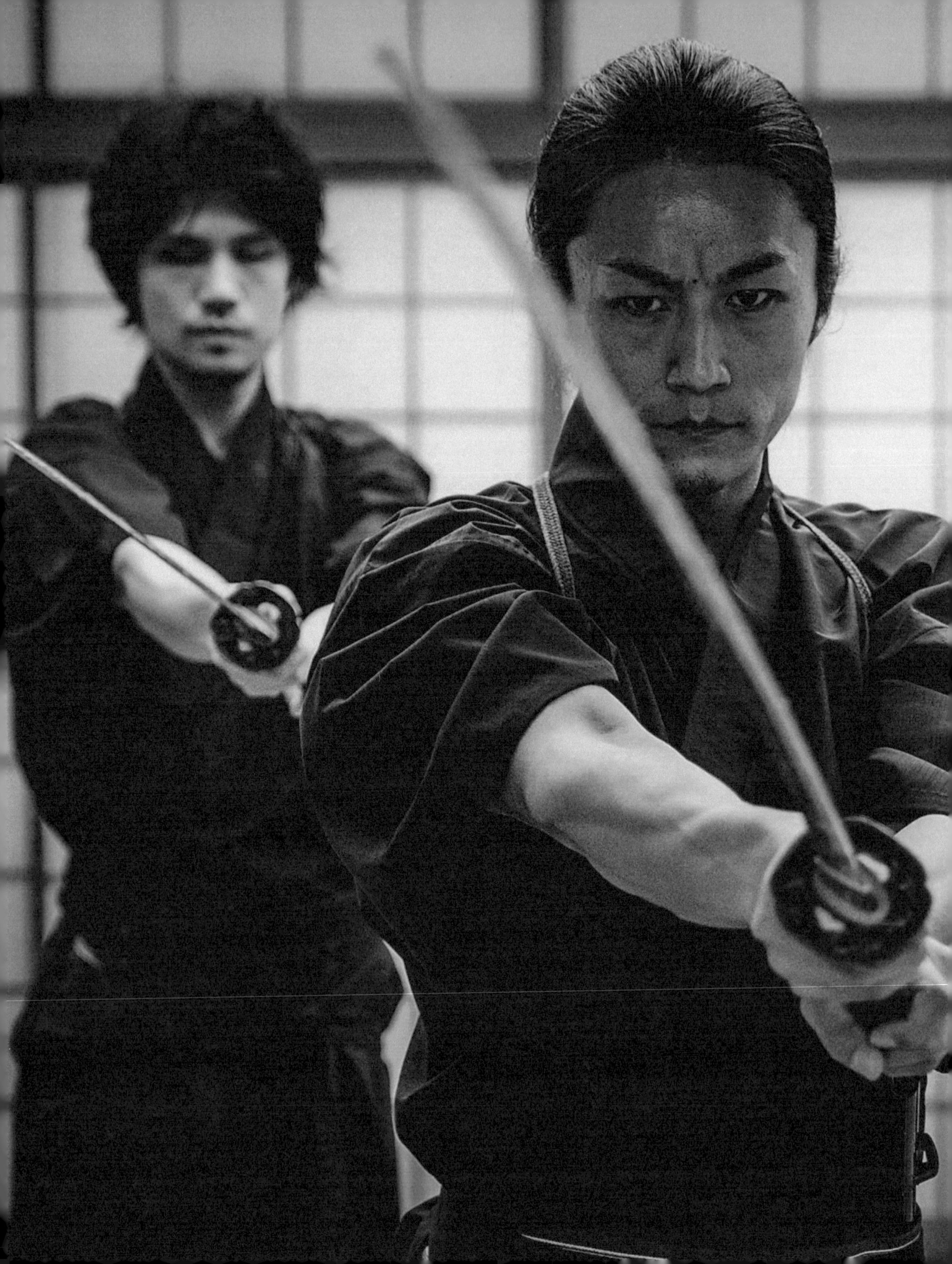

# COURAGE DETERMINATION AND BRAVERY

---
"True courage is not the willingness to die nobly, but the willingness to live proudly and honourably." - Shusaku Endo

---

This quote by Shusaku Endo emphasises that true courage is not solely demonstrated through acts of heroism or martyrdom but rather by living with pride and honour. The author suggests that living with courage requires constant practice and cultivating virtuous thoughts and actions. Endo highlights the importance of living a life that is true to one's values, both in public and private, and that true courage must be embodied in one's innermost being. In essence, this quote speaks to the idea that true courage and integrity are found in living a life that is consistently aligned with one's values rather than simply in moments of bravery or self-sacrifice.

Easy to write. But in practice, we must display the courage to persist in our new way of thinking and being.

We have to work at it. And work constantly and diligently. Whenever we try to change an old pattern, the old pattern fights back. It will reassert itself. So we keep trying until one day, that pattern is broken. Every day will get easier. It's not an easy process, but every day of 'trying' makes a difference. We can't fail unless we stop trying.

Embodying courage in different areas of our lives requires conscious effort and a daily practice. But these practices aren't hard. They just need your determination and willingness to live your best life.

Here are some practices, meditations, and approaches to awaken courage in four different arenas:

## At Home

Take the initiative: Courage often involves taking action, even when it's uncomfortable or scary. Take the initiative to address issues in your family, such as conflicts or challenges.

Stand up for what is right: If you witness something that goes against your values or principles, speak up and take action to address it, even if it's complicated.

Face your fears: Identify any fears or anxieties that are holding you back in your personal life, and work on facing them directly.

Challenge yourself: Try new things, step outside of your comfort zone, and push yourself to do something you may have been afraid to do in the past.

Visualise success: Visualise yourself successfully facing your fears or taking courageous actions, and use this visualisation to build confidence.

Practice gratitude: Focus on what you're grateful for in your life, and use this gratitude to build resilience and courage.

## At Work

Take risks: Courage in the workplace may involve taking calculated risks, such as speaking up in a meeting or proposing a new idea.

Speak truth to power: If you see something that's not right in your workplace, have the courage to speak up, even if it means challenging those in positions of authority.

Stand up for your colleagues: If you witness a colleague being mistreated or unfairly treated, have the courage to support and advocate for them.

Lead by example: Demonstrate courage in your leadership style by taking responsibility for mistakes, being transparent, and standing up for what is right.

Empower others: Encourage and empower those around you to take risks, challenge the status quo, and be courageous in their own lives.

Communicate effectively: Use clear and respectful communication to build trust and foster a culture of courage and authenticity within your team or organisation.

## In Our Relationships

Set healthy boundaries: Have the courage to set healthy boundaries in your relationships, even if it means saying "no" or standing up for yourself.

Take emotional risks: Courage in relationships can mean being vulnerable and sharing your true feelings and emotions with your partner, even when it's uncomfortable.

Challenge old patterns: If you have unhealthy habits in your relationships, have the courage to challenge them and make positive changes.

Communicate assertively: Have the courage to speak up for yourself respectfully and assertively. This means expressing your needs, wants, and feelings clearly and honestly without resorting to passive-aggressiveness or aggression.

Embrace forgiveness: Courage in relationships can mean having the courage to forgive others, even when they have hurt you deeply. This requires vulnerability, compassion, and a willingness to let go of resentment and anger.

Practice empathy: Have the courage to put yourself in your partner's shoes and understand their perspective, even when it's difficult. This means practising empathy, active listening, and non-judgmental communication.

Face your fears: If you have fears or anxieties that are affecting your relationships, have the courage to face them head-on. This means being honest with yourself and your partner about your fears and seeking professional help if needed.

Take responsibility: Be courageous to take responsibility for your actions and apologise when you hurt someone. This means acknowledging your mistakes, making amends, and committing to positive change.

Prioritise self-care: Courage in relationships means having the courage to prioritise your own well-being and self-care. This means setting healthy boundaries, taking time for yourself, and prioritising your physical, emotional, and mental health.

## In a Spiritual Sense

Take action: Courage in a spiritual sense can mean taking action to make positive changes in your life, such as practising self-reflection, forgiveness, or service to others.

Be true to your beliefs: Have the courage to stand up for what you believe in, even if it's unpopular or goes against the norm.

Face your spiritual fears: Identify any spiritual fears or anxieties that are holding you back, and work on facing them directly, with the support of a spiritual community if needed.

## Meditations to Embody Courage

### Short meditation

### 5-10 minutes daily

**A Grounding Courage meditation, in which you focus on grounding yourself in the present moment and finding the courage to face any challenges that come your way.**

Step 1: Find a comfortable and quiet place: Start by finding a comfortable and quiet place where you can sit or lie down without being disturbed. You can sit cross-legged on the floor or in a chair with your feet flat on the ground.

Step 2: Take a deep breath: Take a deep breath in through your nose and exhale slowly through your mouth. Repeat this a few times until you feel relaxed and centred.

Step 3: Visualise roots growing from your feet: Imagine that roots are growing from the soles of your feet and are extending deep into the earth. Visualise these roots wrapping around rocks and stones, anchoring you firmly to the ground.

Step 4: Focus on your breath: Shift your attention to your breath and focus on the sensation of air moving in and out of your body. As you breathe in, imagine that you are inhaling courage and strength. As you breathe out, imagine that you are releasing any doubts or fears.

Step 5: Repeat a grounding affirmation: Repeat a grounding affirmation to yourself, such as "I am grounded, strong, and centred" or "I have the courage to face any challenge that comes my way". Say this affirmation with conviction and believe in its truth.

Step 6: Release tension: Scan your body for any areas of tension or discomfort and release them. If you notice tension in your shoulders, for example, roll them back and down to release the tension.

Step 7: Take another deep breath: Take one final deep breath in through your nose and exhale slowly through your mouth. When you are ready, open your eyes and slowly return to the present moment.

Remember that you can perform this Grounding Courage meditation anytime you need to feel more centred and courageous. It only takes a few minutes and can help you face any challenges that come your way with greater strength and resilience.

## Long Meditation

### 20-30 minutes daily or several times a week.

**A Facing Fear meditation, in which you focus on acknowledging and facing your fears with courage, is a profoundly powerful way to embody deeper levels of determination and bravery**

Step 1: Find a quiet and comfortable place: Find a quiet and comfortable place where you can sit or lie down without being disturbed. You can sit cross-legged on the floor or in a chair with your feet flat on the ground.

Step 2: Set your intention: Set your intention for the meditation. Your intention can be something like "I will face my fears with courage and strength" or "I will acknowledge my fears and release them."

Step 3: Focus on your breath: Close your eyes and take a few deep breaths in through your nose and out through your mouth. Focus on your breath and allow your body to relax with each exhale.

Step 4: Identify your fear: Consider a fear you want to face. It can be a fear of failure, rejection, or anything holding you back from living your life to the fullest.

Step 5: Acknowledge your fear: Acknowledge your fear without judgment or self-criticism. Accept that it is a part of you and that it is okay to feel afraid.

Step 6: Visualise facing your fear: Visualise yourself facing your fear with courage and strength. Imagine yourself overcoming your fear and feeling empowered by your ability to face it.

Step 7: Repeat affirmations: Repeat affirmations to yourself that reinforce your courage and strength. For example, "I am strong, courageous, and capable of facing any fear," or "I release my fear and embrace my inner strength."

Step 8: Release your fear: Release your fear by visualising it leaving your body and mind. Imagine yourself free from the fear and feeling lighter and more empowered.

Step 9: Gratitude: Take a moment to express gratitude for the courage and strength you have within you. Recognise that facing your fear takes courage, and you should be proud of yourself for taking this step.

Step 10: Bring awareness back to your body: Take a few deep breaths and slowly bring your awareness back to your body. Wiggle your toes and fingers, and when you are ready, open your eyes.

Remember, facing fear can be challenging, but with this meditation, you can cultivate the courage and strength to overcome any fear that comes your way.

## Visualisation

**A short visualisation, practised at any time of the day, can be a powerful tool to shift your perspective.**

Imagine yourself standing at the edge of a cliff, facing your fears. Visualise yourself taking a deep breath, feeling grounded and centred, and then taking a courageous leap forward into the unknown.

.

## Affirmations

**Choose a single affirmation you are attracted to or several affirmations, and write them down or memorise them. You can add them to notes around the house. Pin them where you can see them. Chant them to yourself. Sing them. Start the day with some affirmations. Affirmations are a proven way to programme your subconscious, creating profound change.**

I am fearless and confident in the face of any challenge.

I am determined to achieve my goals and will not let fear hold me back.

I am brave and courageous, even in the face of uncertainty.

I trust in my ability to overcome any obstacle that comes my way.

I am strong and resilient, able to handle any situation with grace and ease.

I am worthy of success and will not let fear stop me from achieving it.

I have the courage to step out of my comfort zone and pursue my dreams.

I am bold and daring, willing to take risks to achieve my goals.

I am capable and confident in my ability to handle any challenge.

My courage and determination empower me, and I will not let fear hold me back.

I embrace challenges as opportunities to grow and evolve, and I face them with courage and determination.

I trust that my inner strength and resilience will guide me through any obstacle or adversity I may encounter.

I am a warrior of light, and my courage shines bright even in the darkest of moments.


Affirmations can be a powerful tool for cultivating courage and bravery in our lives. Regularly repeating positive statements to ourselves can shift our mindset and beliefs about our abilities and potential. Affirmations can help us break through limiting beliefs and self-doubt, allowing us to step outside our comfort zones and take risks.

Incorporating affirmations into our daily practice can be particularly helpful for those times when we feel fearful or uncertain. By repeating statements such as "I am brave and capable," "I have the courage to face any challenge," or "I trust myself to handle difficult situations," we can begin to reprogramme our minds to approach challenges with confidence and resilience. Affirmations can help us to cultivate a sense of inner strength and courage that can serve us in all areas of our lives, from personal relationships to career goals. And confidence, ultimately leading to a more fulfilling and satisfying life.

Embodying courage in our lives is a powerful and transformative process that requires deep inner work and commitment. It involves stepping outside of our comfort zones and facing our fears head-on, even when the outcome is uncertain. Courage can be demonstrated in many different ways, such as speaking up for oneself or others, taking risks, standing up for what is right, or facing adversity with grace and resilience. Through the practice of embodying courage, we can cultivate a deeper sense of self-awareness, confidence, and inner strength that can help us overcome challenges and live a more fulfilling life.

The process of embodying courage can be challenging, but the rewards are immeasurable. It begins with an honest examination of ourselves, our values, and our fears. We must be willing to acknowledge our vulnerabilities and limitations while also recognising our potential and strengths. This requires a great deal of self-reflection and introspection, as well as a willingness to take risks and embrace uncertainty. As we practice embodying courage, we may encounter setbacks or failures, but these can be powerful learning opportunities that can help us grow and evolve. Ultimately, embodying courage allows us to live a more authentic and fulfilling life, where we can pursue our passions and dreams with confidence and resilience.

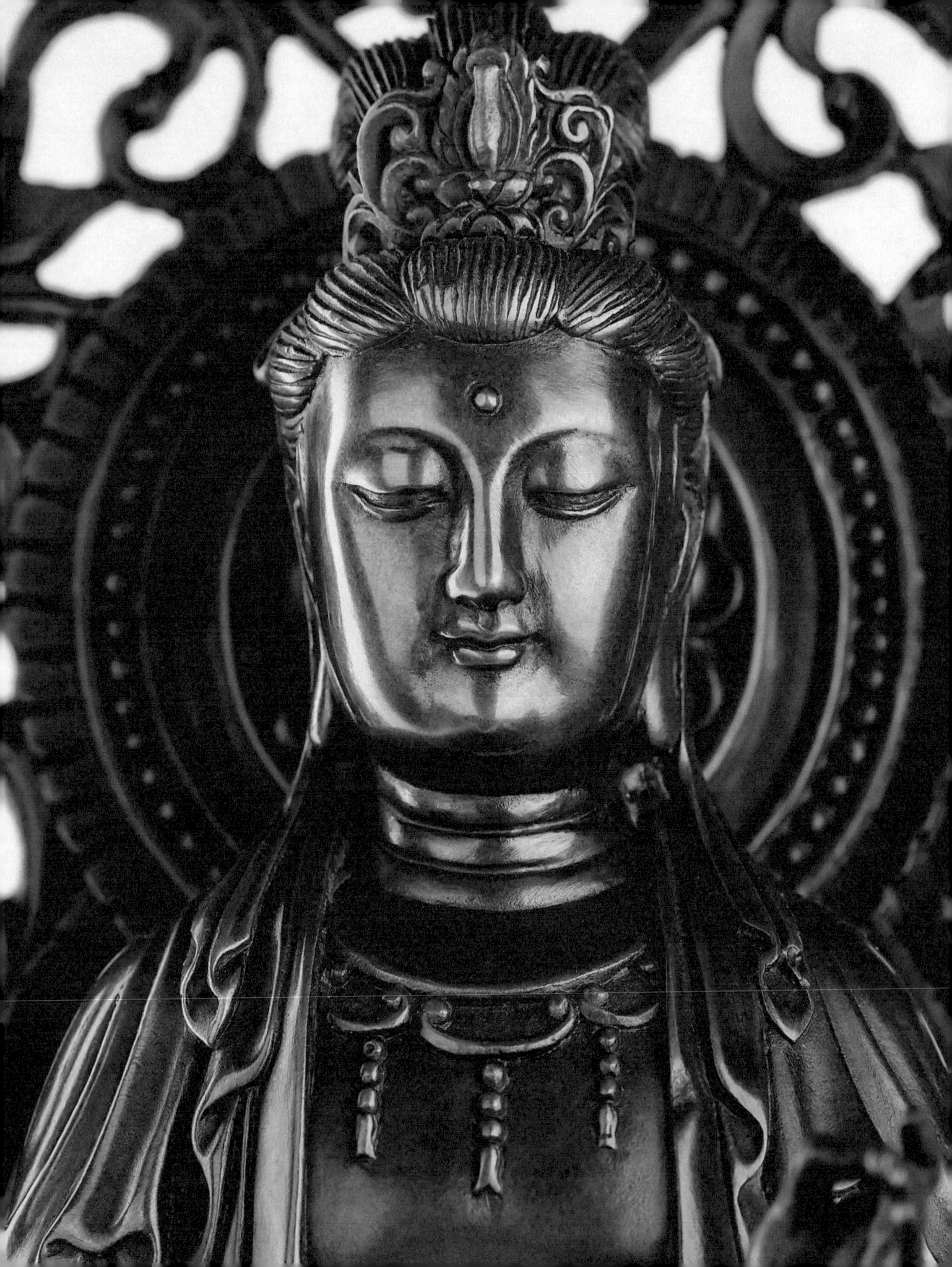

# BENEVOLENCE COMPASSION AND KINDNESS

---

"Humans are saved by other humans"- Ryunosuke Satoro

---

This quote by Ryunosuke Satoro highlights the fundamental interdependence of human beings and the importance of helping and supporting each other in our personal and collective growth and development. It suggests that we cannot thrive or survive alone and that we need each other to overcome challenges and obstacles in life.

At its core, this quote speaks to the power of human connection and the positive impact we can have on each other's lives. It encourages us to extend a helping hand to others in need, to be kind and compassionate, and to foster a sense of community and collaboration. By doing so, we not only benefit the individuals we help but also contribute to creating a more supportive, empathetic, and harmonious society.

In practical terms, Satoro reminds us that we have the ability to make a positive difference in the world, no matter how small our actions may seem. It encourages us to be mindful of the needs and struggles of others, to listen with empathy, and to offer our support in whatever way we can.

This quote also speaks to the idea that we are all connected and that our actions have a ripple effect that can impact others in ways we may never fully understand. By acting with kindness and compassion, we help others and contribute to creating a more positive and supportive world.

It can be hard to introduce greater compassion into our lives, especially when surrounded by people or situations that challenge us and make us feel bad about ourselves or others. It's tough. Nobody said it would be easy. If it *were* easy, everyone would do it. But it becomes easier the more we do it. It's actually far more straightforward than we think. As the Nike slogan says, we just have to do it.

Here are some practices to help you embody benevolence and compassion in different areas of your life:

## At Home

Practice empathy: Try to understand and feel what your family members are experiencing. Show compassion and kindness, especially during difficult times.

Show appreciation: Express gratitude and appreciation to your loved ones for the things they do, even if they're small.

Be helpful: Look for ways to be helpful and kind to your family members, especially when they are in need.

Offer to help with household chores, such as cooking, cleaning, or running errands.

Plan a surprise for your family members, such as organising a fun activity or preparing their favourite meal.

Practice forgiveness and let go of past grudges or misunderstandings.

## At Work

Be a good listener: Listen to your colleagues without judgment or interruption. Try to understand their perspective and show empathy.

Help others: Look for opportunities to help your co-workers with their work or to lend an ear when they need someone to talk to.

Show kindness: Do small acts of kindness, such as offering a compliment or bringing in treats for your co-workers.

Participate in team-building activities to build stronger relationships with your colleagues.

Organise a volunteer event or donation drive with your co-workers to give back to the community.

Support and mentor newer colleagues to help them grow in their roles.

## In Our Relationships

Practice active listening: Listen to your partner without distraction, and try to understand their feelings and perspective.

Show empathy: Try to feel your partner's feelings and show compassion during difficult times.

Be generous: Give your partner your time, energy, and resources without expecting anything in return.

Take the time to provide emotional support to your loved ones when needed.

Write a letter expressing your appreciation and gratitude for your partner or friend.

Offer to help your loved ones with a project or task they are struggling with.

## In a Spiritual Sense

Practice self-compassion: Be kind and understanding towards yourself, and treat yourself as you would a friend.

Show kindness to others: Do small acts of kindness, such as donating to charity or volunteering in your community.

Practice forgiveness: Let go of grudges and forgive others and yourself.

Spend time in nature to connect with the world around you and feel a sense of gratitude and awe.

Practice meditation or prayer to cultivate a sense of inner peace and compassion towards yourself and others.

Help those in need.

## Meditations to Embody Benevolence and Compassion

### Short meditation

### 5-10 minutes daily

**A Compassionate Breath meditation, in which you focus on your breath and breathe in the intention of compassion for yourself and others.**

Step 1: Find a comfortable and quiet place: Begin by finding a comfortable and quiet place where you can sit or lie down without being disturbed. Make sure you won't be interrupted during your meditation.

Step 2: Sit in a comfortable position: Sit in a comfortable position with your back straight and your feet flat on the ground. You can sit on a cushion or a chair, whichever feels more comfortable for you.

Step 3: Take a deep breath: Take a few deep breaths in through your nose and out through your mouth. Allow your breath to become slow and deep. Focus on the sensation of air moving in and out of your body.

Step 4: Set your intention: As you inhale, set your intention to cultivate compassion for yourself and others. Imagine that you are breathing in love and kindness and breathing out any negativity or self-doubt.

Step 5: Visualise compassion: As you continue to breathe, visualise compassion as a bright light or energy that fills your body with warmth and love. Allow this energy to expand beyond yourself and out into the world, touching the lives of others.

Step 6: Repeat a compassionate affirmation: Repeat a compassionate affirmation to yourself, such as "May I be happy, may I be healthy, may I be peaceful" or "May all beings be free from suffering, may all beings be filled with love and compassion". Say this affirmation with sincerity and conviction.

Step 7: Release tension: Scan your body for any areas of tension or discomfort and release them. If you notice tension in your shoulders, for example, roll them back and down to release the tension.

Step 8: Take another deep breath: Take one final deep breath in through your nose and exhale slowly through your mouth. When you are ready, open your eyes and slowly return to the present moment.

Remember that you can perform this Compassionate Breath meditation anytime you need to cultivate more compassion for yourself and others. It can help you cultivate a greater sense of inner peace, kindness, and connection to the world around you

### Long Meditation

*20-30 minutes, or longer, daily or several times a week.*

**A Loving Kindness or Metta meditation, in which you focus on bringing loving kindness to yourself and the world and all beings in it.**

Step 1: Find a comfortable and quiet place: Find a comfortable and quiet place where you can sit or lie down without being disturbed. Sit cross-legged on the floor or in a chair with your feet flat on the ground.

Step 2: Take a few deep breaths: Take a few deep breaths and relax your body. As you exhale, let go of any tension or stress.

Step 3: Focus on your heart centre: Focus your attention on your heart centre, the area in the centre of your chest. Imagine a warm and radiant light glowing in this area.

Step 4: Repeat a loving-kindness phrase: Repeat a loving-kindness phrase or mantra silently to yourself. A common phrase used in Metta meditation is "May I be happy, may I be healthy, may I be peaceful, may I be loved." Repeat this phrase or a similar one, visualising the light in your heart centre growing brighter with each repetition.

Step 5: Expand your focus to others: Once you feel a sense of warmth and love for yourself, expand your focus to others. Picture someone you love, such as a family member or close friend, and repeat the loving-kindness phrase for them. Then, visualise other people in your life, gradually expanding to include people you may have more complicated relationships with or even people you don't know well.

Step 6: Extend loving-kindness to all beings: Once you have included all people in your life, extend the loving-kindness to all beings everywhere. Picture the light in your heart centre radiating out to the world, embracing all living beings with love and compassion.

Step 7: End the meditation: When you're ready, slowly bring your attention back to your surroundings. Take a few deep breaths and feel the warmth and love in your heart centre. Carry this feeling of compassion with you as you go about your day.

Metta loving-kindness meditation is a powerful practice that can help cultivate feelings of love and compassion towards oneself and others. It can also help reduce feelings of anger, resentment, and other negative emotions. With regular practice, Metta meditation can transform how you relate to yourself and the world around you, leading to greater happiness and fulfilment in life.

## Visualisation

**A short visualisation, practised at any time of the day, can be a powerful tool to shift your perspective.**

Imagine yourself surrounded by a warm, loving, and compassionate light. Visualise this light enveloping you and extending out to all beings, radiating love and compassion to all.

## Affirmations

**Choose a single affirmation you are attracted to or several affirmations, and write them down or memorise them. You can add them to notes around the house. Pin them where you can see them. Chant them to yourself. Sing them. Start the day with some affirmations. Affirmations are a proven way to programme your subconscious, creating profound change.**

I am filled with love and compassion for myself and others.

My heart is open and I radiate kindness wherever I go.

I choose to see the good in others and extend kindness without judgment.

I am a force of positivity, and my actions create a ripple effect of kindness.

I am grateful for every opportunity to show kindness and make a positive impact on others.

I am worthy of giving and receiving love, kindness, and compassion.

My kindness and compassion bring joy and happiness to those around me.

I forgive myself and others with compassion and understanding.

I approach every situation with a loving and compassionate heart.

I am a source of love, kindness, and compassion, and I am making the world a better place with my actions.

I am an embodiment of love and my actions reflect this truth.

I choose to see the divine in everyone, and my interactions are guided by this perspective.

I am filled with an abundance of love, and I share it freely with those around me.

I approach every situation with empathy and understanding, seeking to connect with others on a deeper level.

My heart is open to giving and receiving love, and I am grateful for every opportunity to express it.

I am kind and compassionate to myself, and I extend this same kindness to others.

I hold space for others to express their emotions and experiences with love and compassion.

I recognise that we are all on a journey of growth and learning, and I approach others with compassion and patience.

My words and actions are rooted in love and kindness, and I am making a positive impact on the world.

I am a channel for divine love and compassion, and I radiate this energy to all those around me.


Affirmations can be a powerful tool for cultivating compassion and love in our lives. Regularly repeating positive statements to ourselves can shift our mindset and beliefs about our abilities and potential. Affirmations can help us break through limiting beliefs and self-doubt, allowing us to step outside our comfort zones and take risks. Affirmations are a powerful tool to reprogramme our subconscious minds.

Embodying benevolence and compassion in our lives is a process that requires intentional effort and practice. It involves cultivating a genuine care and concern for others and the world around us. To embody benevolence and compassion, we must first begin by recognising the interconnectedness of all beings and developing a deep sense of empathy towards others. We can then engage in daily practices that help us cultivate kindness, generosity, and patience towards ourselves and others. This can include daily acts of kindness, mindful meditation, and volunteering our time and resources to help those in need. With consistent effort and practice, we can begin to embody benevolence and compassion in our everyday lives, leading to a greater sense of inner peace and fulfilment.

The importance of embodying benevolence and compassion in our lives cannot be overstated. These virtues are essential to building meaningful relationships with others, fostering a sense of community, and promoting a more harmonious world. When we embody benevolence and compassion, we create a ripple effect that can positively impact the lives of those around us. Our actions and attitudes towards others can inspire others to do the same, leading to a greater sense of interconnectedness and empathy in our communities. Moreover, embodying benevolence and compassion can also have a profound impact on our own well-being, leading to greater inner peace, happiness, and a sense of purpose.

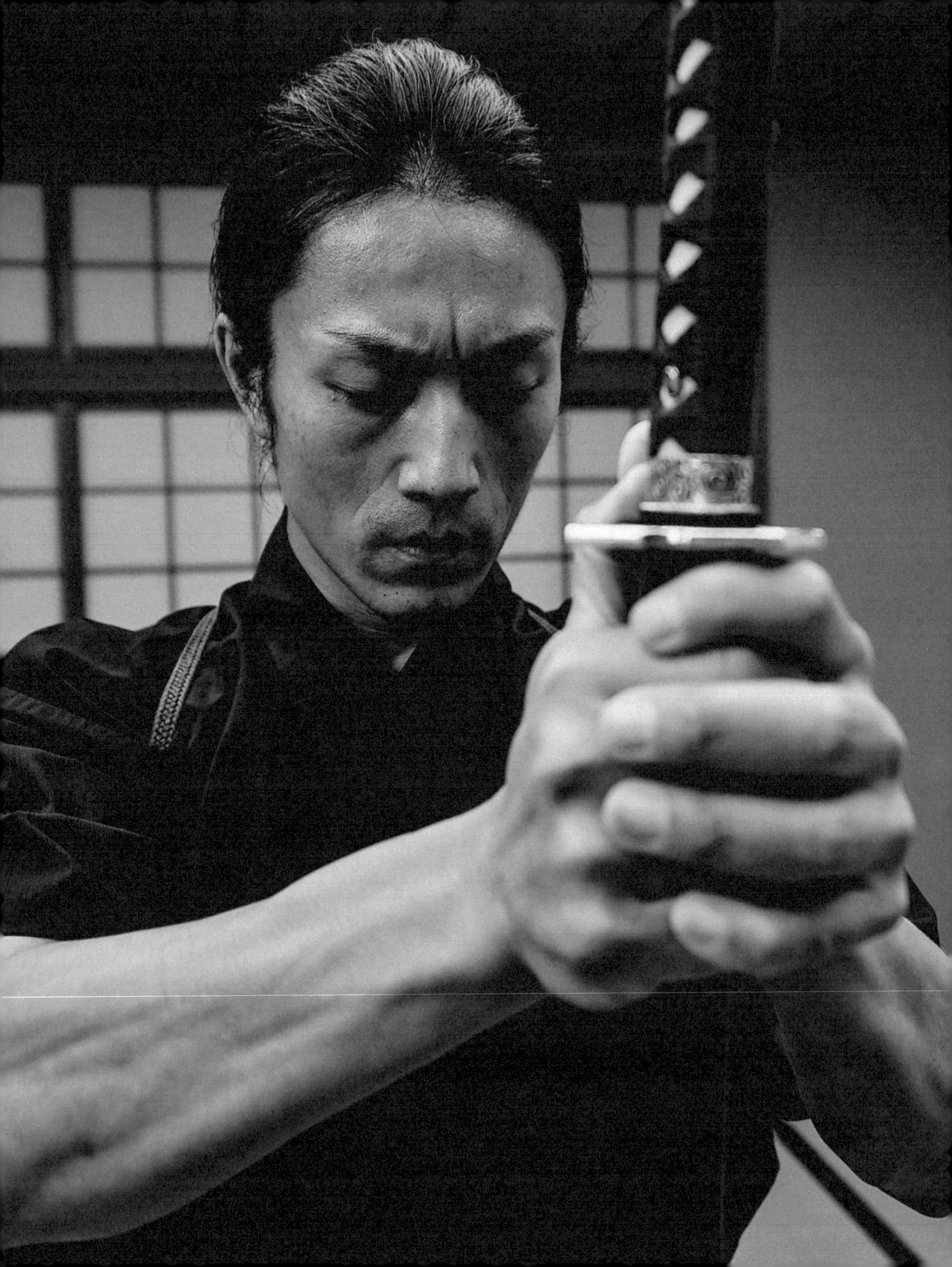

# RESPECT
## EMPATHY AND UNDERSTANDING

*"Do not forget to have a respectful heart"* – Traditional Japanese Saying

This quote emphasises the importance of respect in our interactions with others and reminds us that we should always strive to maintain a sense of respect in our daily lives.

In the 21st century, our society has become increasingly diverse and interconnected. With the rise of technology and social media, our interactions with others have become more frequent and varied, but they also have become less personal and face-to-face. In this context, it is easy to forget about the importance of respect and to prioritise our own needs and desires over the needs and feelings of others.

However, the quote reminds us that respect is a fundamental value that should guide our behaviour and interactions with others. It encourages us to cultivate a respectful heart, which means valuing the dignity and worth of all individuals, regardless of their background, culture, or beliefs. Having a respectful heart involves treating others with kindness, empathy, and understanding, even when we disagree with them or when their actions or opinions differ from ours.

In practical terms, having a respectful heart means being mindful of our words and actions, listening to others with an open mind, and striving to create an environment of mutual respect and understanding. It also means treating ourselves with respect by valuing our own needs and boundaries and recognising that we deserve to be treated with dignity and compassion.

Ultimately, this quote reminds us that respect is not just a nice-to-have value but an essential one that is necessary for creating a healthy, harmonious, and flourishing society. We can create a more compassionate, empathetic, and understanding world by cultivating a respectful heart and prioritising respect in our daily lives.

Let's look at some practices to embody respect in our lives:

## At Home

Show appreciation: Express gratitude and appreciation for your family members' contributions to the household, even for small things like washing the dishes or taking out the trash.

Listen actively: Listen to your family members without interrupting or judging them, and try to understand their perspective.

Practice kindness: Treat your family members with kindness and respect, even during disagreements or difficult times.

Offer to help with household chores, such as cooking, cleaning, or grocery shopping, without being asked.

Be punctual and respect your family members' time by arriving on time for family events or gatherings.

Respect privacy by knocking on closed doors before entering and avoiding eavesdropping on conversations.

## At Work

Communicate respectfully: Use respectful language and tone of voice when communicating with your colleagues, even if you disagree with them.

Acknowledge others' contributions: Show appreciation for your colleagues' contributions and ideas, and give credit where it is due.

Treat everyone equally: Treat all colleagues respectfully, regardless of their position or status.

Practice active listening by paraphrasing your colleagues' words to ensure you understand their perspectives.

Be mindful of your body language and tone of voice when interacting with your colleagues to convey respect and openness.

Avoid interrupting your colleagues during meetings or conversations, and wait for your turn to speak.

## In Our Relationships

Honour boundaries: Respect your partner's boundaries and communicate your own clearly.

Practice empathy: Try to understand your partner's perspective and feelings, even if they differ from yours.

Avoid judgment: Avoid judging or criticising your partner, and instead, offer constructive feedback and support.

## In a Spiritual Sense

Practice non-judgment: Avoid judging others based on their beliefs, and instead strive to understand and respect different perspectives.

Show reverence: Show reverence for the natural world, and treat it with respect and care.

Practice humility: Cultivate humility and recognise that you are not the centre of the universe. Be open to learning from others and new experiences.

Practice gratitude: Practice gratitude for the blessings in your life, recognising the interconnectedness of all things and the role that others have played in your journey.

Seek understanding: Seek to understand different perspectives and worldviews, recognising that we are all interconnected and that our differences reflect the diversity and richness of the universe.

Honour the sacred: Honour the sacred in all things, recognising the inherent divinity of all beings and their role in the unfolding of the universe.

## Meditations to Embody Respect

### Short meditation

### 5-10 minutes daily

**A Respectful Breathing meditation, in which you focus on your breath and breathe in the intention of respect for yourself and others.**

Step 1: Find a comfortable and quiet place: Begin by finding a comfortable and quiet place where you can sit or lie down without being disturbed. Make sure you won't be interrupted during your meditation.

Step 2: Sit in a comfortable position: Sit in a comfortable position with your back straight and your feet flat on the ground. You can sit on a cushion or a chair, whichever feels more comfortable for you.

Step 3: Take a deep breath: Take a few deep breaths in through your nose and out through your mouth. Allow your breath to become slow and deep. Focus on the sensation of air moving in and out of your body.

Step 4: Set your intention: As you inhale, set your intention to cultivate respect for yourself and others. Imagine breathing in respect and breathing out any judgment or negativity towards yourself or others.

Step 5: Visualise respect: As you continue to breathe, visualise respect as a golden light or energy that fills your body with warmth and appreciation. Allow this energy to expand beyond yourself and out into the world, touching the lives of others.

Step 6: Repeat a respectful affirmation: Repeat a respectful affirmation to yourself, such as "I respect myself and others, as we are all deserving of respect" or "May all beings be treated with respect and kindness". Say this affirmation with sincerity and conviction.

Step 7: Release tension: Scan your body for any areas of tension or discomfort and release them. If you notice tension in your shoulders, for example, roll them back and down to release the tension.

Step 8: Take another deep breath: Take one final deep breath in through your nose and exhale slowly through your mouth. When you are ready, open your eyes and slowly return to the present moment.

Remember that you can perform this Respectful Breath meditation anytime you need to cultivate more respect for yourself and others. It can help you cultivate a greater sense of inner peace, understanding, and connection to the world around you.

## Long Meditation

### 30-40 minutes, or longer, daily or several times weekly.

**A Respect for All meditation, in which you focus on cultivating a deep sense of respect for all beings.**

Step 1: Find a comfortable and quiet place: Begin by finding a comfortable and quiet place where you can sit or lie down without being disturbed. Make sure you won't be interrupted during your meditation.

Step 2: Sit in a comfortable position: Sit in a comfortable position with your back straight and your feet flat on the ground. You can sit on a cushion or a chair, whichever feels more comfortable for you.

Step 3: Take a deep breath: Take a few deep breaths in through your nose and out through your mouth. Allow your breath to become slow and deep. Focus on the sensation of air moving in and out of your body.

Step 4: Set your intention: As you inhale, set your intention to cultivate a deep sense of respect for all beings. Imagine that you are breathing in respect and breathing out any judgment or negativity towards yourself or others.

Step 5: Visualise respect: As you continue to breathe, visualise respect as a glowing light or energy that fills your body with warmth and appreciation. Allow this energy to expand beyond yourself and out into the world, touching the lives of all beings.

Step 6: Practice loving-kindness: Begin by directing loving-kindness towards yourself. Repeat the phrase "May I be filled with love, kindness, and respect" several times, allowing the feeling of love and respect to grow within you.

Step 7: Expand to loved ones: Next, direct loving-kindness towards loved ones. Repeat the phrase "May my loved ones be filled with love, kindness, and respect" several times, picturing their faces and feeling deep respect for them.

Step 8: Expand to acquaintances: Next, direct loving-kindness towards acquaintances. Repeat the phrase "May my acquaintances be filled with love, kindness, and respect" several times, picturing their faces and feeling deep respect for them.

Step 9: Expand to all beings: Finally, direct loving-kindness towards all beings. Repeat the phrase "May all beings be filled with love, kindness, and respect" several times, picturing all beings worldwide and feeling a deep respect for them.

Step 10: Cultivate empathy: Take a moment to imagine the struggles and challenges all beings face and cultivate a sense of empathy towards them. Imagine how you would feel in their place and how you can show respect to them.

Step 11: Reflect on respect: Take some time to reflect on what respect means to you and how you can cultivate a more profound sense of respect towards all beings in your daily life.

Step 12: Release tension: Scan your body for any areas of tension or discomfort and release them. If you notice tension in your shoulders, for example, roll them back and down to release the tension.

Step 13: Take another deep breath: Take one final deep breath in through your nose and exhale slowly through your mouth. When you are ready, open your eyes and slowly return to the present moment.

Remember that you can perform this Respect for All meditation anytime you need to cultivate more respect for all beings. It can help you cultivate a greater sense of empathy, understanding, and connection to all beings in the world around you.

## Visualisation

**A short visualisation, practised at any time of the day, can be a powerful tool to shift your perspective.**

Imagine yourself standing in a beautiful forest, surrounded by trees of all shapes and sizes. Visualise yourself feeling a deep sense of respect for the trees and the natural world around you, recognising their inherent value and importance.

.

## Affirmations

**Choose a single affirmation you are attracted to or several affirmations, and write them down or memorise them. You can add them to notes around the house. Pin them where you can see them. Chant them to yourself. Sing them. Start the day with some affirmations. Affirmations are a proven way to programme your subconscious, creating profound change.**

I treat myself and others with kindness, compassion, and respect.

I recognise and honour the inherent worth and dignity of all beings.

I choose to speak and act with respect towards myself and others.

I listen attentively and with an open mind to others' perspectives and ideas.

I am committed to creating a safe and inclusive space for all beings.

I value diversity and appreciate the unique qualities and experiences of all beings.

I am worthy of respect and will not tolerate any form of disrespect towards myself or others.

I acknowledge and take responsibility for my own biases and work to overcome them.

I communicate assertively and respectfully, with the intention of building understanding and connection.

I am grateful for the contributions of all beings and show appreciation and respect for them.

I am committed to creating positive change in the world through respectful and compassionate action.

I trust in the power of respect to heal relationships and bring people closer together.

I embrace the interconnectedness of all beings and recognise that by respecting others, I am also respecting myself.


Affirmations are a powerful tool for cultivating respect in our lives. We can shift our mindset and behaviours to align with this virtue by repeating positive statements and beliefs to ourselves. Incorporating affirmations into our daily practice can help us embody respect in all aspects of our lives, from how we treat ourselves to others.

Through affirmations, we can reinforce the importance of respecting ourselves, our boundaries, and the dignity and worth of those around us. By regularly reminding ourselves of the value and importance of respect, we can cultivate a deep sense of empathy and compassion for others, even in difficult situations. Affirmations can also help us stay mindful and present in our interactions, so we can more easily recognise and respond to opportunities to show respect and kindness to ourselves and others.

---

Embodying respect is a lifelong journey that requires consistent effort and mindfulness. It involves acknowledging the inherent worth of every individual and treating them accordingly. Practicing kindness, empathy, and humility on a daily basis can help you embody this value and make it a core part of your being.

Respect also involves being open-minded and willing to learn from others, regardless of their background, experience, or position in life. It means recognising the value and contributions of every individual, regardless of their race, gender, religion, sexual orientation, or socio-economic status.

And embodying respect requires a deep commitment to social justice and equity. It means actively working towards dismantling systems of oppression and discrimination and promoting equality and inclusion for all. This involves speaking up against injustice, supporting marginalised communities, and educating oneself and others about the issues facing our society.

---

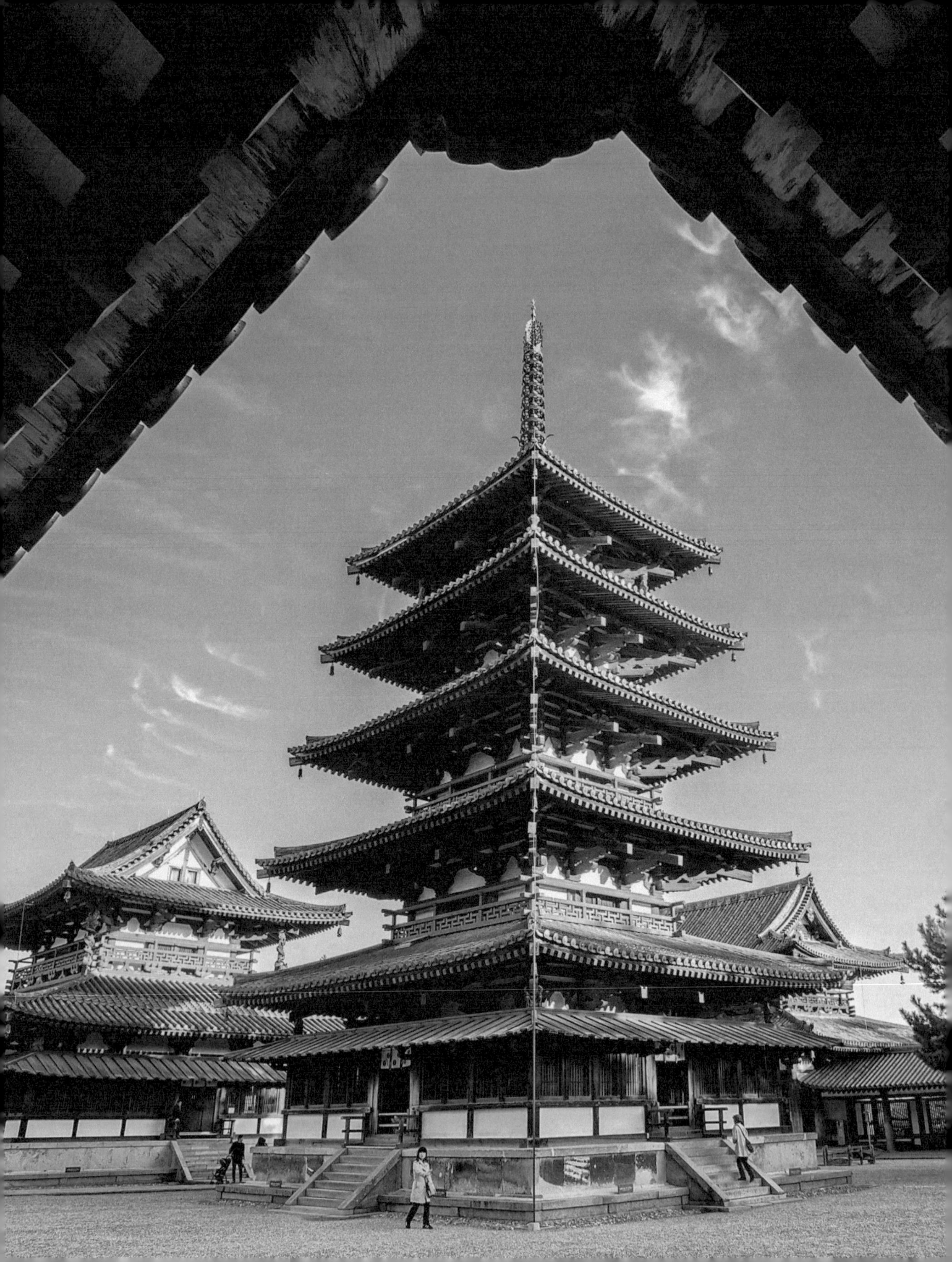

# HONESTY TRUST AND INTEGRITY

---

"Know your faults. Once you know your faults, do not hide them" – Popular Japanese Saying

---

The Japanese quote "己の欠点を知れ。欠点を知りて、欠点を隠すことなかれ (Onore no ketten wo shire. Ketten wo shirite, ketten wo kakusu koto nakare) is a powerful reminder of the importance of self-awareness, honesty, and integrity in one's personal and professional life.

At its core, the quote encourages individuals to be honest with themselves about their weaknesses and mistakes. Rather than ignoring or denying these faults, the quote urges individuals to confront them directly and to take steps towards improving themselves. This approach requires humility, courage, and a willingness to learn and grow from one's experiences.

Additionally, the quote emphasises the importance of transparency and openness in relationships. By acknowledging and openly discussing one's faults, individuals can build trust and respect with others. Concealing or hiding one's weaknesses, on the other hand, can lead to misunderstandings, mistrust, and negative consequences in personal and professional relationships.

Overall, the quote reflects a fundamental value in Japanese culture of striving for self-improvement and integrity in all aspects of life. By embracing this value and committing to self-awareness, honesty, and transparency, individuals can build stronger, more meaningful relationships with others and lead more fulfilling lives.

Let's take a look at some simple practices to help us embody honesty in our lives

## At Home

Speak honestly: Communicate honestly and openly with your family members, even if difficult or uncomfortable.

Keep your promises: Keep your promises and commitments to your family members, and follow through on your word.

Be reliable: Show up on time and be reliable, so your family members can trust you.

## At Work

Be truthful: Communicate honestly and truthfully with your colleagues, even when it's challenging.

Keep confidential information confidential: Respect the confidentiality of sensitive information and don't share it with others.

Honour your commitments: Follow through on your commitments and deliver on your promises to build trust with your colleagues.

Be transparent: Be transparent in your communication with colleagues and managers, sharing information openly and honestly to build a culture of trust.

Practice active listening: Practice active listening to understand your colleagues' perspectives and show that you value their opinions.

Avoid gossip: Avoid gossip or negative talk about others and instead focus on building positive relationships based on trust and respect.

Own up to mistakes: Take responsibility for your mistakes and be accountable for your actions so that colleagues can trust you to do the right thing.

Respect boundaries: Respect the boundaries of your colleagues and avoid crossing personal or professional lines that may compromise trust.

Share credit: Share credit and recognition for successes with your colleagues, demonstrating that you value their contributions and building a culture of trust and respect.

## In Our Relationships

Communicate clearly: Communicate clearly and openly with your partner, and listen actively to understand their perspective.

Show consistency: Be consistent in your behaviour and actions, so your partner can trust you.

Be loyal: Be loyal to your partner and honour your commitments to build trust in your relationship.

Practice transparency: Practice transparency in your communication with your partner, sharing your thoughts, feelings, and intentions openly and honestly.

Honour your agreements: Honour your agreements with your partner, and follow through on your commitments to build a sense of reliability and trust.

Cultivate empathy: Cultivate empathy for your partner, seeking to understand their perspective and feelings even when they differ from yours.

Be accountable: Take responsibility for your actions and mistakes, and make amends when necessary to rebuild trust in your relationship.

## In a Spiritual Sense

Practice self-reflection: Reflect on your thoughts and actions, and strive to align them with your values and beliefs.

Be honest with yourself: Be honest with yourself about your motivations and intentions, and strive to act with integrity.

Build trust with the divine: Cultivate a trusting relationship with a higher power through prayer, meditation, and acts of service.

Let go of falsehoods: Release any false beliefs or illusions holding you back from living in alignment with your true self and values.

## Meditations to Embody Honesty and Trust

### Short meditation

### 5-10 minutes daily

**An Honesty Breathing meditation, in which you focus on your breath and breathe in the intention of sincerity and trust.**

Step 1: Find a comfortable and quiet place: Begin by finding a comfortable and quiet place where you can sit or lie down without being disturbed. Make sure you won't be interrupted during your meditation.

Step 2: Sit in a comfortable position: Sit in a comfortable position with your back straight and your feet flat on the ground. You can sit on a cushion or a chair, whichever feels more comfortable for you.

Step 3: Take a deep breath: Take a few deep breaths in through your nose and out through your mouth. Allow your breath to become slow and deep. Focus on the sensation of air moving in and out of your body.

Step 4: Set your intention: As you inhale, set your intention to cultivate honesty and trust. Imagine that you are breathing in sincerity and breathing out any doubts or falsehoods.

Step 5: Visualise honesty: As you continue to breathe, visualise honesty as a bright light or energy that fills your body with clarity and truth. Allow this energy to expand beyond yourself and out into the world, helping to inspire others to live with integrity and honesty.

Step 6: Repeat a sincere affirmation: Repeat a sincere affirmation to yourself, such as "I trust myself and my intuition" or "I am living in alignment with my true values and beliefs". Say this affirmation with sincerity and conviction.

Step 7: Release tension: Scan your body for any areas of tension or discomfort and release them. If you notice tension in your shoulders, for example, roll them back and down to release the tension.

Step 8: Take another deep breath: Take one final deep breath in through your nose and exhale slowly through your mouth. When you are ready, open your eyes and slowly return to the present moment.

Remember that you can perform this Honesty Breathing meditation anytime you need to cultivate more sincerity and trust in your life. It can help you cultivate a greater sense of inner peace, clarity, and authenticity.

### Long Meditation

*30-40 minutes, or longer, daily or several times weekly.*

**A Building Trust meditation, in which you focus on building trust within yourself and with others.**

Step 1: Find a comfortable and quiet place: Begin by finding a comfortable and quiet place where you can sit or lie down without being disturbed. Make sure you won't be interrupted during your meditation.

Step 2: Set your intention: As you begin your meditation, set your intention to cultivate trust within yourself and with others. Imagine that you are breathing in trust and breathing out any doubts or fears.

Step 3: Focus on your breath: Take a few deep breaths and allow your breath to become slow and deep. Focus on the sensation of air moving in and out of your body.

Step 4: Visualise trust: As you continue to breathe, visualise trust as a bright light or energy that fills your body with warmth and security. Allow this energy to expand beyond yourself and out into the world, touching the lives of others.

Step 5: Practice forgiveness: Consider any past hurts or betrayals that may have eroded your trust in others. Practice forgiveness for these past experiences, and release any lingering resentment or anger.

Step 6: Practice honesty: Reflect on any areas in your life where you may have been less than truthful or honest. Commit to being more honest and transparent in your words and actions moving forward.

Step 7: Practice vulnerability: Acknowledge any fears or insecurities you may have about being vulnerable with others. Practice opening up and sharing your thoughts and feelings with those you trust.

Step 8: Cultivate compassion: Cultivate compassion for yourself and others, recognising that building trust takes time and effort. Be patient with yourself and others as you work to deepen your relationships.

Step 9: Repeat a trust-affirming mantra: Repeat a trust-affirming mantra to yourself, such as "I trust myself and others" or "I am worthy of trust and respect". Say this affirmation with sincerity and conviction.

Step 10: Release tension: Scan your body for any areas of tension or discomfort and release them. If you notice tension in your shoulders, for example, roll them back and down to release the tension.

Step 11: Take another deep breath: Take one final deep breath in through your nose and exhale slowly through your mouth. When you are ready, open your eyes and slowly return to the present moment.

Remember that you can perform this Building Trust meditation anytime you need to cultivate more trust within yourself and with others. It can help you deepen your connections with others and cultivate a greater sense of inner peace and security.

## Visualisation

**A short visualisation, practised at any time of the day, can be a powerful tool to shift your perspective.**

Imagine yourself standing in a clear, calm ocean, representing the depth of your honesty and trust. Visualise yourself diving down into the depths of the ocean, exploring the beauty and mystery of the unknown.

## Affirmations

**Choose a single affirmation you are attracted to or several affirmations, and write them down or memorise them. You can add them to notes around the house. Pin them where you can see them. Chant them to yourself. Sing them. Start the day with some affirmations. Affirmations are a proven way to programme your subconscious, creating profound change.**

I choose honesty and trust as the foundation of my relationships.

I am worthy of trust and respect, and I extend the same to others.

My integrity and honesty bring me peace and clarity of mind.

I am committed to being truthful and trustworthy in all areas of my life.

Trust is built through consistent honesty, and I am committed to consistency.

I honour my commitments and follow through on my promises.

I listen with an open heart and communicate with sincerity and authenticity.

I trust my intuition and act with integrity in all situations.

Honesty and transparency are the keys to building strong, healthy relationships.

I choose to speak my truth with kindness and compassion.

I forgive myself for past dishonesty and commit to a future of honesty and trust.

Trust is the foundation of all healthy relationships, and I am committed to building and nurturing trust in my life.

I speak my truth with courage and conviction, even in the face of challenge or opposition.

I am honest with myself about my strengths, weaknesses, and areas for growth.

My honesty and integrity attract positive and trustworthy people into my life.

I am accountable for my actions and take responsibility for my mistakes with honesty and grace.

I trust that being truthful and authentic will always lead me to the right path and the right people.


To fully embody honesty, integrity, and trust, it is essential to integrate these affirmations into your daily routine with consistency and purpose. Repeating these affirmations regularly will help you internalise them and make them a natural part of your thought process.

Make a conscious effort to incorporate these affirmations into your daily practice, such as reciting them during meditation, repeating them in front of a mirror, or writing them down in a journal. By consistently reminding yourself of these positive affirmations, you can gradually shift your mindset and behaviour towards greater honesty, integrity, and trustworthiness. Remember that true transformation takes time and effort, so be patient and persistent in your practice.

Embodying honesty and trust is essential for living a fulfilling and authentic life. When we are honest with ourselves and others, we build a foundation of trust that can support deeper and more meaningful relationships. Honesty allows us to show up authentically in the world, while trust enables us to rely on others and be relied upon in turn. Embodying these qualities requires consistent effort and commitment, but the rewards are immeasurable.

The process of embodying honesty and trust involves both inner and outer work. Internally, we must be willing to reflect on our thoughts and actions, and examine our motivations and intentions. This can be uncomfortable, as we may uncover aspects of ourselves that we don't want to face. However, it is only through this process of self-reflection that we can gain a deeper understanding of our own truth and align our actions with our values. Externally, embodying honesty and trust requires that we communicate openly and truthfully with others, keep our commitments, and respect the confidentiality of sensitive information. It also involves being vulnerable and transparent in our relationships, showing up authentically and being willing to listen and learn from others. Through consistent practice, we can cultivate a deeper sense of honesty and trust in our lives, leading to more fulfilling and connected relationships with ourselves and others.

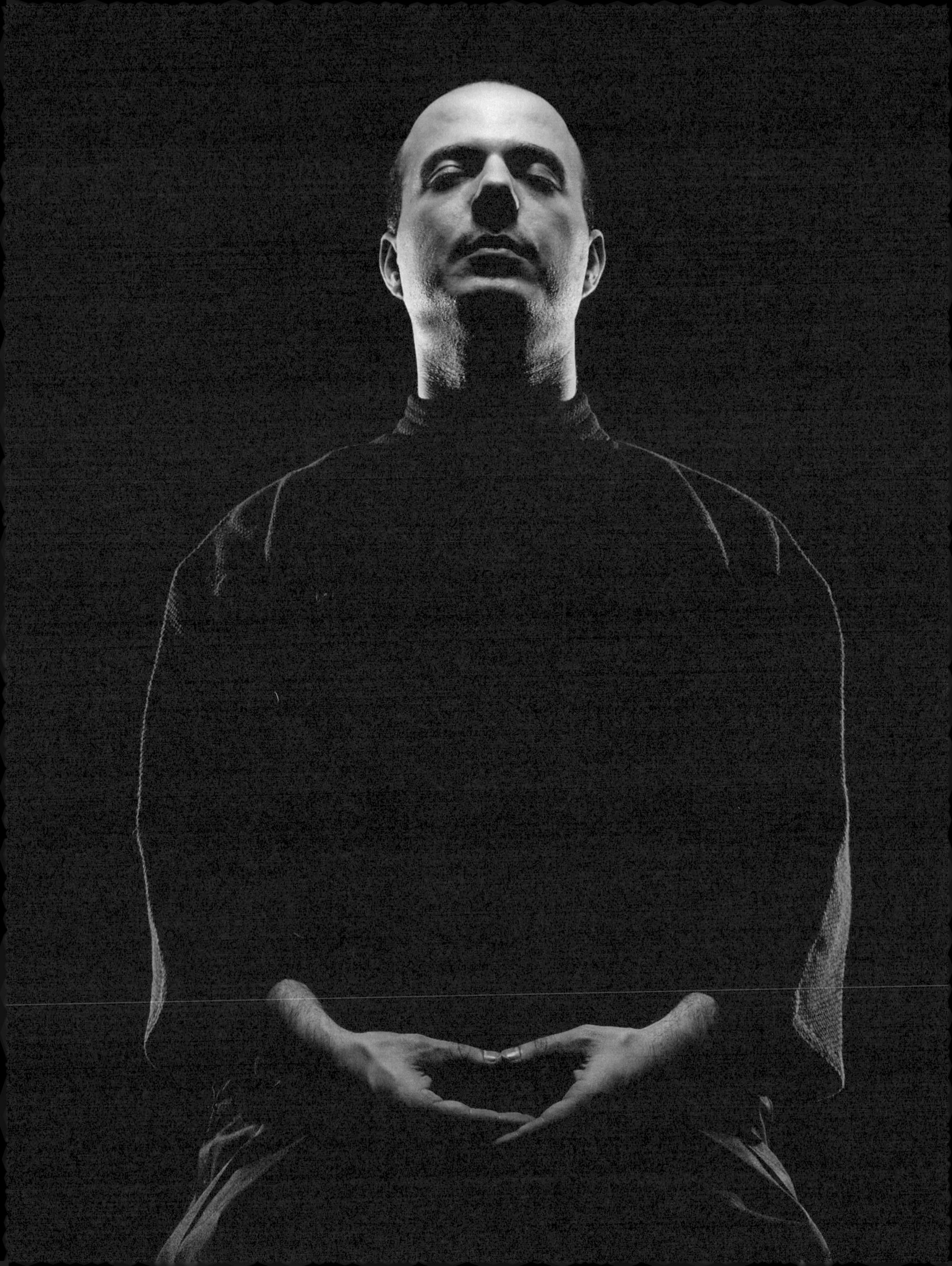

# HONOUR INTEGRITY AND TRUTH

---

"Those who possess truth and justice are always enveloped in honour." – Traditional Japanese Saying

---

The Japanese quote "真実と正義を持つ人は、いつも名誉に包まれている (Shinjitsu to seigi wo motsu hito wa, itsumo meiyo ni tsutsumarete iru) emphasises the importance of truth, justice, and integrity in achieving honour. It suggests that individuals who embody these values will always be enveloped in honour, regardless of their external circumstances. At its core, the quote highlights the role of character and ethics in personal and professional life.

In the 21st century, this quote remains relevant as society grapples with ongoing ethical leadership and accountability challenges. With information and communication more accessible than ever, the importance of upholding truth and justice has become increasingly apparent. By prioritising these values, individuals and communities can build a culture of trust, respect, and honour.

The quote also implies that honour cannot be easily earned or bought but rather a quality that is earned through consistent adherence to one's principles and values. It reflects one's character and how one conducts oneself in all life aspects.

So this quote serves as a reminder that honour is not merely a product of external achievements or status but a reflection of one's inner qualities and values. By upholding truth, justice, and integrity in all aspects of life, individuals and communities can build a culture of trust, respect, and honour.

Let's take a look at how we can start to embody honour in our lives

## At Home

Be respectful: Show respect to your family members, even during disagreements or conflicts.

Keep your promises: Follow through on your commitments and keep your promises to your family members.

Be a role model: Set a positive example for your family members by embodying honourable behaviour and values.

Apologise when you are wrong: Acknowledge your mistakes and apologise to your family members when you hurt or let them down.

Show gratitude: Express gratitude and appreciation to your family members for their support, kindness, and love.

Avoid gossip: Refrain from gossiping or speaking negatively about your family members behind their backs.

## At Work

Act with integrity: Make ethical decisions and act with integrity, even when it's difficult or unpopular.

Take responsibility: Take responsibility for your actions and admit when you make mistakes.

Be accountable: Be accountable to your colleagues and hold yourself to a high standard of professionalism and ethical behaviour.

Respect diversity: Embrace diversity and differences in opinion, culture, and background, and treat all colleagues with respect.

Speak up against unethical behaviour: Speak up against unethical behaviour or practices in the workplace, and be a voice of integrity.

Share credit: Give credit where it's due and acknowledge the contributions of others.

## In Our Relationships

Practice empathy: Try to understand your partner's feelings and perspective, and treat them with respect and dignity.

Keep your word: Honour your commitments and follow through on your promises to your partner.

Be loyal: Be loyal and faithful to your partner, and avoid behaviours that could compromise their trust in you.

Be forgiving: Practice forgiveness and let go of grudges, resentment, and anger towards your partner.

Prioritise communication: Prioritise open, honest, and respectful communication in your relationship, and actively listen to your partner's needs and concerns.

Respect personal space: Respect your partner's personal space and allow them to have their own time and interests.

## .In a Spiritual Sense

Cultivate self-awareness: Reflect on your values and beliefs, and strive to align your behaviour with them.

Serve others: Serve others with honour and respect, and be mindful of how your actions impact the world around you.

Seek wisdom: Seek wisdom and guidance from spiritual leaders and texts, and strive to live a life of purpose and meaning.

Practice gratitude: Cultivate a sense of appreciation for the blessings in your life, and appreciate the beauty and wonder of the world around you.

Serve the community: Serve your community through volunteering, charity work, or other forms of service, and honour your responsibility towards others.

Practice mindfulness: Practice mindfulness through meditation, yoga, or other practices, and be present in the moment with awareness and compassion.

Remember that embodying honour requires a daily practice of ethical behaviour, accountability, and self-reflection. Be patient with yourself and others, and strive to live a life of integrity and purpose. By embodying honour in all aspects of your life, you can positively impact the people and environment around you.

## Meditations to Embody Honesty and Trust

### Short meditation

### 5-10 minutes daily

**An Honourable Breathing meditation, in which you focus on your breath and breathe in the intention of honour.**

Step 1: Find a quiet and comfortable place: Begin by finding a quiet and comfortable place where you won't be disturbed. Choose a location where you can sit or lie down without any distractions. Make sure that you can relax and breathe deeply.

Step 2: Sit in a comfortable position: Sit in a comfortable position with your back straight, your feet flat on the ground, and your hands resting on your knees or in your lap. Choose a place that feels comfortable for you, whether it's sitting on a cushion or a chair.

Step 3: Take a few deep breaths: Take a few deep breaths in through your nose and out through your mouth. Allow your breath to become slow and deep. Focus on the sensation of air moving in and out of your body.

Step 4: Set your intention: As you inhale, set your intention to cultivate honour. Imagine that you are breathing in a golden light that represents honour and breathing out any dishonourable thoughts or emotions.

Step 5: Visualise honour: As you continue to breathe, visualise honour as a bright light or energy that fills your body with integrity, respect, and dignity. Allow this energy to expand beyond yourself and out into the world, inspiring others to live with honour.

Step 6: Repeat an honourable affirmation: Repeat an honourable affirmation to yourself, such as "I live with honour and respect for myself and others" or "I make choices that align with my values and honourable principles". Say this affirmation with sincerity and conviction.

Step 7: Release tension: Scan your body for any areas of tension or discomfort and release them. If you notice tension in your shoulders, for example, roll them back and down to release the tension.

Step 8: Take one final deep breath: Take one final deep breath in through your nose and exhale slowly through your mouth. When you are ready, open your eyes and slowly return to the present moment.

Remember that you can perform this Honourable Breathing meditation anytime you need to cultivate more honour in your life. It can help you cultivate a greater sense of inner peace, respect, and dignity.

## Long Meditation

### 30-40 minutes, or longer, daily or several times weekly.

**An Honouring Yourself and Others meditation, in which you focus on cultivating a deep sense of honour for yourself and others.**

Step 1: Find a quiet and comfortable space: Start by finding a quiet and comfortable space where you can relax and focus without any interruptions. This could be a room in your home or a peaceful outdoor location.

Step 2: Get into a comfortable position: Sit or lie down in a comfortable position with your back straight, your shoulders relaxed, and your arms resting by your sides. You can place your hands on your lap or your belly if that helps you relax.

Step 3: Take a few deep breaths: Close your eyes and take a few deep breaths, inhaling through your nose and exhaling through your mouth. As you breathe, allow your body to relax and release any tension or stress.

Step 4: Set your intention: As you inhale, set the intention to cultivate a deep sense of honour for yourself and others. Imagine breathing in a warm, golden light representing honour and breathing out any negative thoughts or emotions that may be holding you back.

Step 5: Visualise honour: As you continue to breathe deeply, visualise a bright, radiant light that represents honour and respect. Imagine this light filling up your entire body, spreading out to your surroundings, and radiating outwards to encompass all those around you.

Step 6: Honour yourself: Consider a time when you acted with honour, integrity, and dignity towards yourself. Visualise this memory and allow the feelings of pride, self-respect, and self-worth to fill you up. Repeat to yourself "I honour myself for my past actions and my present worth".

Step 7: Honour others: Think of someone in your life whom you admire and respect for their honourable qualities. Visualise their image and allow their positive attributes to inspire feelings of honour and respect within you. Repeat to yourself, "I honour this person and their honourable qualities".

Step 8: Extend honour to others: Expand your feelings of honour and respect outwards to others in your life. Visualise those whom you love and appreciate, and extend your feelings of honour towards them. Wish them well and hope they will experience the same sense of honour and respect you feel.

Step 9: Return to the present: When you're ready, slowly bring your attention back to your breath and your surroundings. Take a deep breath in and slowly exhale out. Open your eyes and take a moment to ground yourself before resuming your day.

## Visualisation

**A short visualisation, practised at any time of the day, can be a powerful tool to shift your perspective.**

Imagine yourself standing on a mountaintop, representing the height of your honour. Visualise yourself feeling a deep sense of reverence and respect for the mountain, recognising its strength and majesty

## Affirmations

**Choose a single affirmation you are attracted to or several affirmations, and write them down or memorise them. You can add them to notes around the house. Pin them where you can see them. Chant them to yourself. Sing them. Start the day with some affirmations. Affirmations are a proven way to programme your subconscious, creating profound change.**

I honour myself by living my truth and following my heart.

I am worthy of respect and honour from others and myself.

I choose to speak and act with integrity and honour.

My actions and words reflect the honour that I hold within me.

I embody honour by treating others with kindness and respect.

I am proud of who I am and the values I stand for.

I honour my commitments and responsibilities.

I trust myself to make honourable choices and decisions.

My life is filled with honour and dignity.

I honour the beauty and sacredness of all life.

My thoughts and beliefs are aligned with my sense of honour and integrity.

I am a person of honour, and I attract honourable people and situations into my life.

I stand firmly in my truth, even when it's unpopular or uncomfortable.

I hold myself to a high standard of integrity and honour in all areas of my life.

My actions and words reflect the deep sense of honour that I hold within me.

I am guided by my inner compass of truth and honour, even in difficult situations.

I honour the truth within myself and others, even when it's difficult or inconvenient.

I choose to live a life of honour, dignity, and respect for myself and others.

I am grateful for the opportunities to express my honour and integrity in the world.

I trust that honour and truth are guiding me on my path to greater fulfilment and happiness.


To fully embody the virtues of honour and truth, it's crucial to incorporate affirmations into your daily practice. Affirmations are most effective when repeated regularly and with intention. By repeating affirmations that focus on honour and truth, you can strengthen your commitment to living a life of integrity.

Consider starting each day with a few moments of reflection, reciting affirmations that resonate with you. Throughout the day, take a few moments to pause and reflect on your intentions, and use affirmations to ground yourself in the virtues of honour and truth. As you practice these affirmations regularly, you'll begin to see changes in your behaviour and find that living a life of integrity becomes second nature. Remember that embodying honour and truth is a lifelong journey, so be patient with yourself and stay committed to your daily practice.

---

Learning to embody honour in our lives is essential for personal growth, self-respect, and cultivating healthy relationships with others. Honour is a fundamental quality that encompasses integrity, respect, and dignity. It involves aligning our thoughts, words, and actions with our inner values and principles. When we embody honour, we show up as our best selves, act with integrity, and earn the respect of others. We are more confident, authentic, and at peace with ourselves.

Embodying honour also has a positive impact on our relationships with others. When we honour ourselves, we set healthy boundaries and communicate our needs and values clearly. This helps us attract and maintain healthy relationships with others who share our values and respect our boundaries. We also learn to treat others with respect, kindness, and empathy, which fosters deeper connections and strengthens our relationships. In addition, embodying honour promotes trust, reliability, and accountability, which are crucial qualities in any relationship. Ultimately, learning to embody honour in our lives helps us live more fulfilling and meaningful lives, where we can be proud of our actions and the impact, we have on others

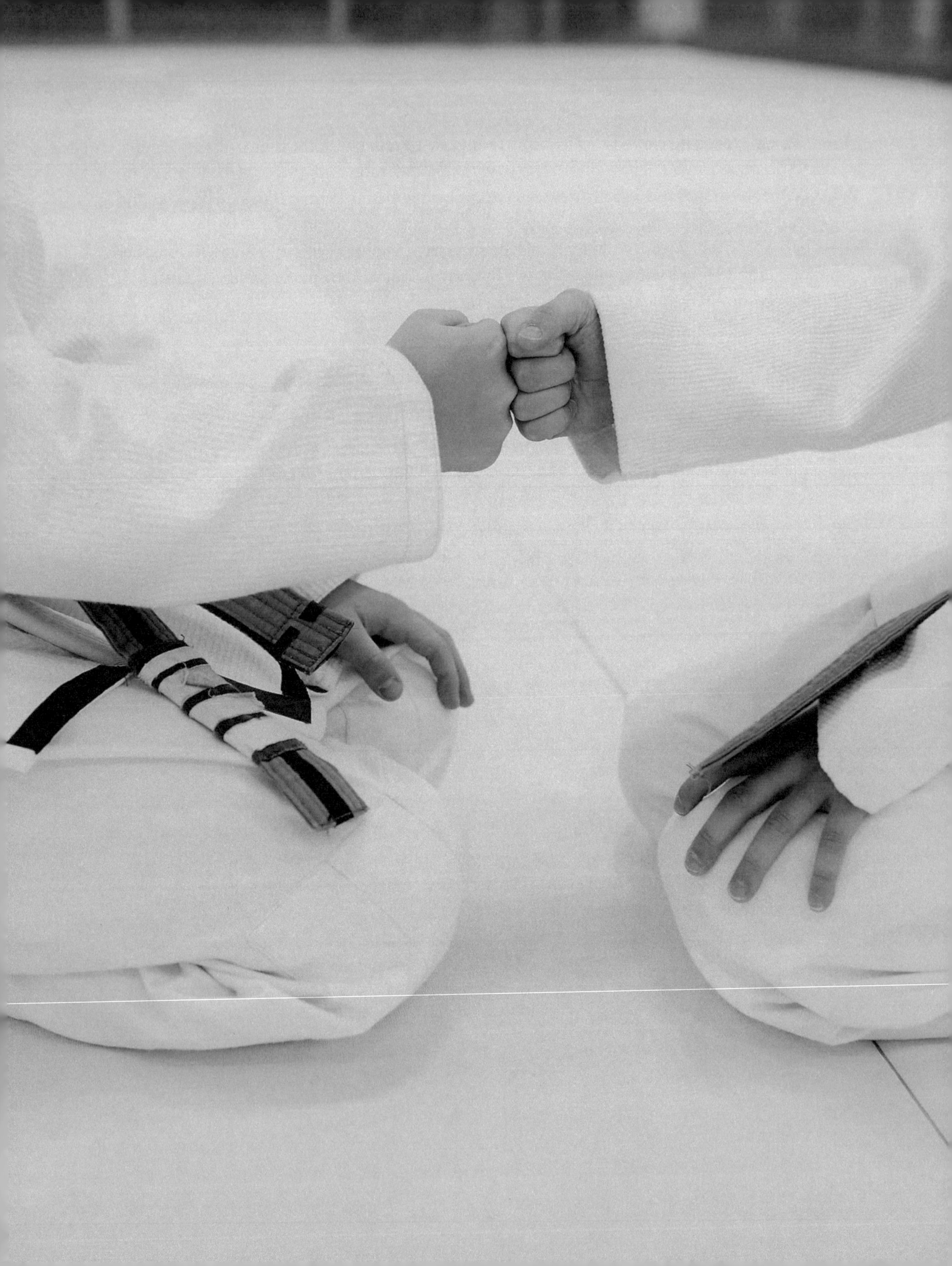

# LOYALTY TRUTH AND TRUST

---

"Loyalty is at the root of human nature" – Popular Japanese Saying

---

The Japanese quote 忠義は人の根本にある (Chuugi wa hito no konpon ni aru), or "Loyalty is at the root of human nature," is a profound statement about the importance of loyalty in human relationships and the human experience.

It suggests that loyalty is not just a desirable trait or a nice-to-have quality but rather a fundamental aspect of being human. This implies that humans are wired to seek and provide loyalty in their relationships with others and that loyalty is a key component of our identity and sense of self.

This quote also suggests that loyalty plays a significant role in our sense of belonging and spiritual growth. In a world that can often feel fragmented and disconnected, loyalty can provide a foundation for strong relationships and a sense of community. By committing ourselves to a cause, a group, or a relationship, we can create a sense of purpose and belonging that can be deeply fulfilling.

The relevance of this quote to the 21st century is clear, as many people today are seeking more meaningful connections and a sense of purpose in their lives. In an era of increasing individualism and social fragmentation, it can be easy to feel disconnected from others and have a sense of meaning and purpose. However, cultivating loyalty in our relationships and communities can build stronger bonds and a greater understanding of connection and belonging.

In addition to its social and emotional benefits, loyalty can also play a key role in our spiritual growth. Many spiritual traditions emphasise the importance of loyalty to a higher power, a community, or a set of ethical principles. By embodying loyalty in our spiritual practices, we can deepen our sense of connection to the divine and strengthen our inner sense of purpose and meaning.

Overall, this quotation speaks to the importance of loyalty as a fundamental aspect of human nature that can provide a foundation for strong relationships, a sense of belonging, and spiritual growth. By cultivating loyalty, we can tap into a deep wellspring of meaning and purpose that can sustain us in even the most challenging times.

Let's take a look at how we can start to embody the quality of loyalty in our lives

## At Home

Be present: Be present and attentive to your family members, and prioritise spending quality time together.

Support one another: Show support and encouragement for your family members, and be there for them during difficult times.

Maintain strong bonds: Work to maintain strong and healthy relationships with your family members, even when it's challenging.

Show up for important events and occasions, such as birthdays or graduations, to demonstrate your loyalty and support.

Be forgiving and understanding of family members' mistakes and shortcomings and offer support to help them grow and improve.

Avoid gossip or negative talk about family members, as this can undermine trust and loyalty in the family.

## At Work

Be a team player: Work collaboratively with your colleagues, and support them in achieving shared goals.

Show commitment: Demonstrate a strong work ethic and commitment to your job and organisation.

Keep confidences: Keep confidential information private and don't share it with others to show loyalty to your colleagues and organisation.

Advocate for your colleagues and their accomplishments and celebrate their successes.

Respect your employer's policies and procedures, even if you don't agree with them, to demonstrate loyalty to the organisation.

Offer to help colleagues struggling with their work, demonstrating your commitment to the team's success.

## In Our Relationships

Show dedication: Demonstrate your dedication and commitment to your partner, and be there for them through thick and thin.

Be trustworthy: Build trust with your partner by being truthful, reliable, and consistent.

Avoid betrayals: Avoid behaviours that could betray your partner's trust, such as infidelity or deceit.

Express your love and appreciation for your partner regularly to reinforce the bond of loyalty between you.

Be open and transparent with your partner about your thoughts and feelings to build a foundation of trust and loyalty.

Prioritise spending time with your partner and making them feel valued and important.

## In a Spiritual Sense

Cultivate devotion: Cultivate a strong sense of devotion and loyalty to your spiritual beliefs and practices.

Serve others: Serve others with loyalty and dedication, and be mindful of how your actions can benefit the world around you.

Show respect: Show respect and reverence for spiritual leaders and texts, and honour their teachings through your actions.

Dedicate time and resources to causes or organisations that align with your spiritual beliefs to demonstrate your loyalty to your values.

Seek out opportunities to learn more about your spiritual beliefs and practices and deepen your understanding and commitment to them.

Share your spiritual journey and insights with others to help inspire and encourage them on their own paths.

Remember that embodying loyalty requires a daily practice of dedication, commitment, and support. Be patient with yourself and others, and strive to be loyal to the people and values that matter most to you. By embodying loyalty in all aspects of your life, you can create deep and meaningful relationships and contribute positively to the world around you.

## Meditations to Embody Honesty and Trust

### Short meditation

### 5-10 minutes daily

**A Loyal Breathing meditation, in which you focus on your breath and breathe in the intention of loyalty.**

Step 1: Find a quiet and comfortable place: Begin by finding a quiet and comfortable place where you can sit or lie down without being disturbed. Make sure that you will not be interrupted during your meditation.

Step 2: Sit in a comfortable position: Sit in a comfortable position with your back straight and your feet flat on the ground. You can sit on a cushion or a chair, whichever feels more comfortable for you.

Step 3: Take a few deep breaths: Take a few deep breaths in through your nose and out through your mouth. Allow your breath to become slow and deep. Focus on the sensation of air moving in and out of your body.

Step 4: Set your intention: As you inhale, set your intention to cultivate loyalty. Imagine that you are breathing in loyalty and breathing out any doubts or feelings of disloyalty.

Step 5: Visualise loyalty: As you continue to breathe, visualise loyalty as a bright light or energy that fills your body with trust and dedication. Allow this energy to expand beyond yourself and out into the world, helping to inspire others to live with loyalty and devotion.

Step 6: Repeat a sincere affirmation: Repeat a sincere affirmation to yourself, such as "I am a loyal friend and partner" or "I show loyalty to myself and others in all that I do". Say this affirmation with sincerity and conviction.

Step 7: Release tension: Scan your body for any areas of tension or discomfort and release them. If you notice tension in your shoulders, for example, roll them back and down to release the tension.

Step 8: Take another deep breath: Take one final deep breath in through your nose and exhale slowly through your mouth. When you are ready, open your eyes and slowly return to the present moment.

Remember that you can perform this Loyal Breathing meditation anytime you need to cultivate more loyalty in your life. It can help you develop a stronger sense of commitment, trust, and dedication to yourself and those around you.

## Long Meditation

### 30-40 minutes, or longer, daily or several times weekly.

**A Cultivating Loyalty meditation, in which you focus on cultivating loyalty to yourself and those you care about.**

A Cultivating Loyalty meditation can help strengthen your bonds with those you care about and create a deep connection and trust. Follow these steps to begin:

Step 1: Find a comfortable and quiet place: Begin by finding a comfortable and quiet place where you can sit or lie down without being disturbed. Make sure you won't be interrupted during your meditation.

Step 2: Sit in a comfortable position: Sit in a comfortable position with your back straight and your feet flat on the ground. You can sit on a cushion or a chair, whichever feels more comfortable for you.

Step 3: Take a deep breath: Take a few deep breaths in through your nose and out through your mouth. Allow your breath to become slow and deep. Focus on the sensation of air moving in and out of your body.

Step 4: Set your intention: As you inhale, set your intention to cultivate loyalty. Imagine that you are breathing in loyalty and breathing out any doubts or fears that may be holding you back from being loyal.

Step 5: Visualise loyalty: As you continue to breathe, visualise loyalty as a bright light or energy that fills your body with a deep sense of connection and trust. Imagine this energy expanding beyond yourself and reaching out to those you care about, strengthening your bond with them.

Step 6: Repeat a sincere affirmation: Repeat a sincere affirmation to yourself, such as "I am loyal to myself and to those I care about" or "I choose to cultivate loyalty in all my relationships". Say this affirmation with sincerity and conviction.

Step 7: Scan your body: Scan your body for any areas of tension or discomfort and release them. If you notice tension in your shoulders, for example, roll them back and down to release the tension.

Step 8: Focus on a specific relationship: Choose a relationship you want to cultivate loyalty in. It could be a friendship, a romantic partnership, or a family member. Imagine the person or people you have chosen and focus on the feeling of loyalty that you would like to cultivate between you.

Step 9: Visualise the relationship: Visualise the relationship between you and the person or people you have chosen. Imagine it becoming stronger, more connected, and filled with trust and loyalty.

Step 10: Repeat your affirmation: Repeat your affirmation again, focusing specifically on the relationship you have chosen. Say it with sincerity and conviction, imagining that it is strengthening your bond with that person or people.

Step 11: Take another deep breath: Take one final deep breath in through your nose and exhale slowly through your mouth. When you are ready, open your eyes and slowly return to the present moment.

Remember that you can perform this Cultivating Loyalty meditation anytime you need to strengthen your connections with those you care about. It can help you cultivate a more profound sense of loyalty, harmony, and trust, creating more fulfilling relationships in your life.

## Visualisation

**A short visualisation, practised at any time of the day, can be a powerful tool to shift your perspective.**

Imagine yourself standing in the centre of a circle of loved ones, representing your loyalty to those you care about. Visualise yourself surrounded by a warm, protective light, symbolising your commitment to standing by your loved ones through thick and thin.

## Affirmations

**Choose a single affirmation you are attracted to or several affirmations, and write them down or memorise them. You can add them to notes around the house. Pin them where you can see them. Chant them to yourself. Sing them. Start the day with some affirmations. Affirmations are a proven way to programme your subconscious, creating profound change.**

I am loyal to myself and to those I care about.

I am a trustworthy and dependable friend.

My loyalty inspires others to be loyal as well.

I am committed to my values and beliefs and remain loyal to them even in difficult times.

I act with integrity and am true to my word, demonstrating loyalty to others.

I cultivate trust and reliability in my relationships through my loyalty.

My loyalty brings strength and stability to my relationships.

I am faithful to my commitments and follow through on my promises.

I am dedicated to supporting and uplifting those I am loyal to.

I prioritise loyalty in my relationships and value it highly.

I am a source of unwavering support and encouragement to those I care about.

My loyalty brings a sense of security and comfort to those around me.

I remain loyal even in challenging circumstances, showing my devotion to others.

I am a beacon of loyalty, inspiring others to be loyal as well.

I express my loyalty through my actions, words, and intentions.

I am committed to building and nurturing trustworthy relationships.

My loyalty and trustworthiness create a foundation of deep connection and intimacy with others.

I am reliable and consistent in my actions, demonstrating my loyalty and trustworthiness.

I honour my commitments and responsibilities, showing my loyalty to others.

I am a person of my word, and my actions reflect my trustworthiness and loyalty.

My loyalty and trustworthiness build a sense of safety and security for those around me.

I choose to see the best in others and trust them until given a reason not to.

My loyalty and trustworthiness create a positive and uplifting environment for those I interact with.

I am committed to being someone others can rely on in both good times and bad.

My loyalty and trustworthiness create strong bonds of friendship and love.

I am confident in my ability to keep confidences and maintain the trust of others.

I consistently demonstrate my loyalty and trustworthiness, earning the respect and admiration of those around me.

I am a loyal and trustworthy ally to those who need support and guidance.

My loyalty and trustworthiness are unwavering, even in the face of challenges or difficulties.

I choose to be a person who inspires trust and loyalty in others, building a strong and supportive community.

Affirmations are a potent tool for cultivating loyalty and trust in your life. When you repeat these affirmations regularly and with intention, you shift your mindset and beliefs towards ones centred on reliability, devotion and faithfulness. Doing so creates a foundation for deep and meaningful connections with yourself and those around you.

Incorporating affirmations into your daily practice is essential for embodying loyalty and trust. By setting aside time each day to repeat these affirmations, you reinforce the values important to you and align your thoughts and actions with them. This can help you become more conscious of your words and deeds, ensuring they align with the principles of faithfulness and dependability. With consistent practice, you can cultivate a deep sense of loyalty and trust, not just in your relationships with others but also in your relationship with yourself.

Do not neglect the power and potential of affirmations. Practiced diligently, they are one of the most powerful tools available for creating change.

Embodying loyalty into our lives is a process that requires practice and dedication. It involves developing a deep sense of commitment to oneself and to others, as well as cultivating a sense of trust and dependability. One important step in this process is learning to set clear boundaries and commitments that align with our values and priorities. This means being honest with ourselves and others about what we are willing and able to commit to, and following through with those commitments even when it may be challenging or uncomfortable. Another important aspect of embodying loyalty is developing a sense of empathy and compassion for others. This means taking the time to truly listen and understand the needs and perspectives of those around us, and being willing to support them through both the good times and the challenging ones.

Learning to embody loyalty into our lives is important for several reasons. First and foremost, it allows us to build strong and meaningful relationships with those around us. When we are loyal and dependable, we create an environment of trust and safety that allows others to feel supported and cared for. This can lead to deeper connections and more fulfilling relationships, both personally and professionally. Additionally, embodying loyalty can help us to live with greater integrity and purpose. When we are clear about our values and commitments, we are better able to make decisions that align with those values and live in a way that feels authentic and true to ourselves. Ultimately, embodying loyalty can help us to cultivate a greater sense of inner peace, fulfilment, and connection with others

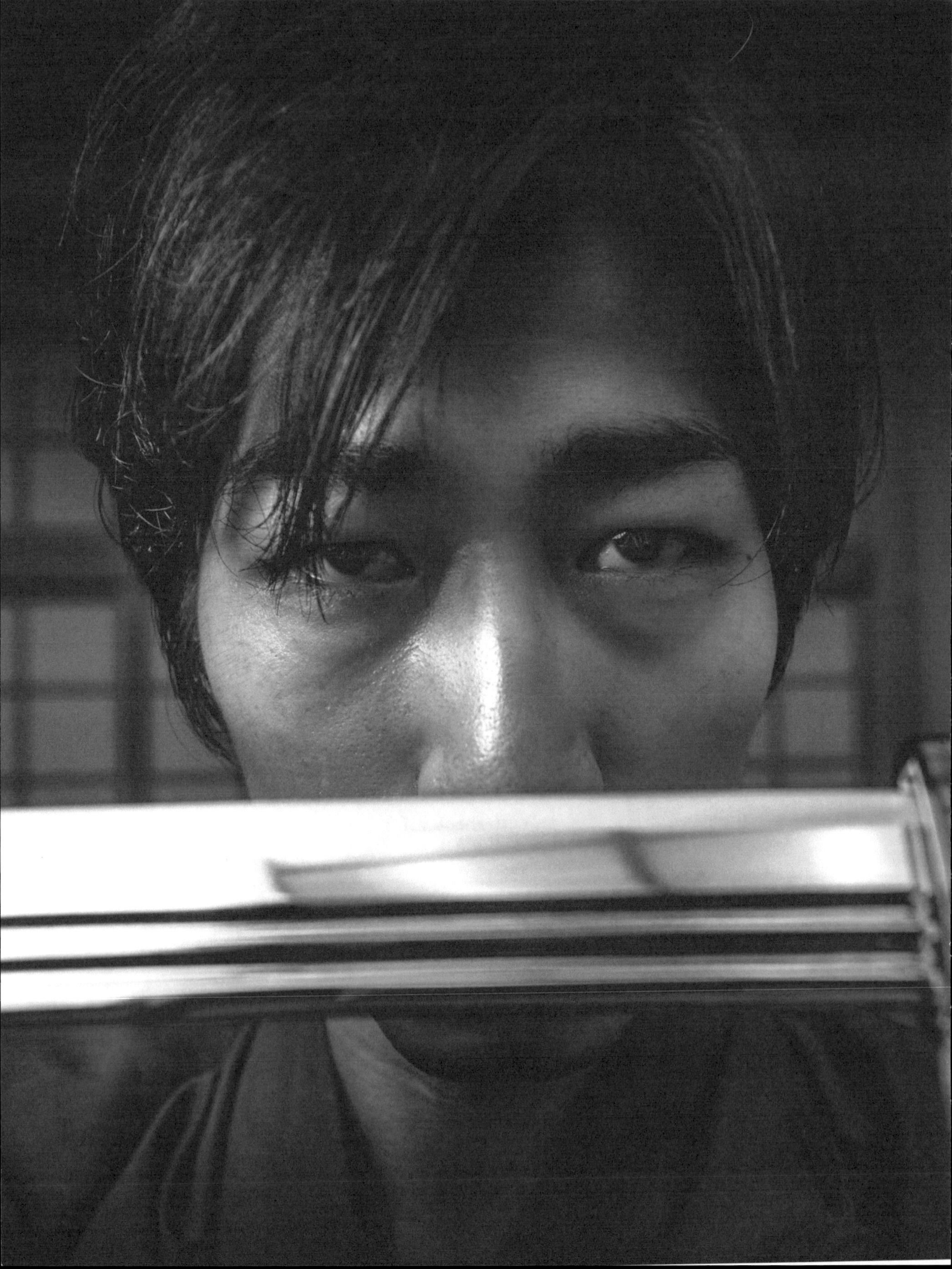

# SELF-CONTROL
## DISCIPLINE AND RESTRAINT

"Self-control is the greatest freedom – Common Japanese Saying

The quote "自己制御こそ最大の自由" (Jiko seigyo koso saidai no jiyuu), which translates to "Self-control is the greatest freedom," highlights the importance of self-discipline in achieving true freedom and happiness.

In our modern world, we are constantly bombarded by temptations and distractions that can derail our efforts to achieve our goals and live our values. Whether it's the lure of instant gratification, the pressure to conform to social norms, or the addictive pull of technology and social media, it can be all too easy to lose control and give in to our impulses.

However, the quote reminds us that true freedom is not simply the ability to do whatever we want without consequences but rather the ability to choose our actions and emotions consciously and intentionally. By exercising self-control, we can break free from the grip of our desires and impulses and make choices that align with our deepest values and aspirations.

Moreover, the quote suggests that self-control is not a static or innate quality but a skill that can be developed and strengthened through practice and discipline. By setting clear goals, establishing healthy habits, and learning to regulate our emotions and impulses, we can cultivate our capacity for self-control and become more resilient, focused, and effective in achieving our goals.

At the same time, the quote recognises that self-control is not always easy. It can be a difficult and sometimes painful process, requiring us to confront our fears, weaknesses, and limitations. It may involve making difficult choices and sacrifices, such as giving up unhealthy habits or breaking away from toxic relationships.

However, the quote suggests that the rewards of self-control are well worth the effort. By developing our capacity for self-control, we can become more empowered and fulfilled in all areas of our lives. We can experience a greater sense of agency and purpose as we learn to direct our energies and choices in a way that serves our highest good and the greater good.

Overall, this quote emphasises the importance of self-discipline and self-restraint in achieving true freedom and happiness. By developing our capacity for self-control, we can become more empowered, focused, and effective in achieving our goals and living our values.

Let's explore some practices to embody the virtue of Self-Control in our lives

## At Home

Practice mindfulness: Practice mindfulness meditation to become more aware of your thoughts and emotions and to help manage them more calmly.

Manage your impulses: Identify any impulsive behaviours that are not serving you or your family well, and work on managing them through self-control techniques.

Set boundaries: Set healthy boundaries with family members to avoid overextending yourself and to prevent unnecessary conflict.

Practice delayed gratification: Delay gratification by resisting temptations or impulses that may have negative consequences in the long run.

Practice self-talk: Use positive self-talk to boost your self-control and motivation when faced with difficult situations.

Practice self-care: Take care of your physical and emotional well-being to promote better self-control and resilience.

## At Work

Manage your time: Plan your workday and prioritise your tasks to avoid feeling overwhelmed and to maintain focus.

Avoid distractions: Avoid distractions such as social media or email during work hours to stay on task and focused on your goals.

Manage your stress: Practice stress management techniques, such as deep breathing or taking short breaks when you feel overwhelmed, to maintain a sense of self-control in the workplace.

Practice goal setting: Set specific and achievable goals to help you stay focused and motivated in your work.

Practice self-monitoring: Keep track of your progress and performance to stay accountable and motivated towards achieving your goals.

Practice delegation: Delegate tasks to others when possible to avoid becoming overwhelmed and to maintain better self-control.

## In Our Relationships

Practice empathy: Practice empathy and try to see situations from others' perspectives to avoid reacting impulsively and promote healthy communication.

Control your temper: Work on managing your emotions and avoiding angry outbursts, to maintain healthy relationships with others.

Set healthy boundaries: Set healthy boundaries in your relationships to prevent yourself from being taken advantage of or becoming overly enmeshed in others' issues.

Practice forgiveness: Forgive yourself and others for mistakes or shortcomings and let go of resentments to promote healthier relationships.

Practice active listening: Listen actively and attentively to others to avoid misunderstandings and to promote empathy and understanding.

Practice flexibility: Be open-minded and flexible in your relationships to avoid rigid thinking and promote better problem-solving.

## In a Spiritual Sense

Practice self-reflection: Take time to reflect on your spiritual beliefs and values and identify areas where you need to exercise greater self-control.

Practice self-discipline: Incorporate spiritual practices, such as fasting or abstaining from certain activities, to cultivate greater self-discipline and self-control.

Seek guidance: Seek guidance from spiritual leaders or texts to learn more about self-control and to find inspiration for developing this virtue.

Practice gratitude: Cultivate a sense of gratitude and appreciation for the blessings in your life to promote greater self-control and positivity.

Practice mindfulness in daily activities: Practice mindfulness during meditation and daily activities to cultivate greater self-awareness and control over your thoughts and actions.

Practice self-forgiveness: Forgive yourself for mistakes or shortcomings in your spiritual practice, and use them as opportunities for growth and learning.

Remember that self-control requires a daily practice of self-awareness, self-discipline, and mindfulness. Be patient with yourself and others, and strive to maintain a sense of calm and balance in all aspects of your life. By embodying self-control, you can improve your relationships, reduce stress, and live a more fulfilling life

## Meditations to Embody Honesty and Trust

### Short meditation

### 5-10 minutes daily

**A Breathing for Self-Control meditation, in which you focus on your breath and breathe in the intention of self-control.**

Step 1: Find a comfortable and quiet space: Begin by finding a comfortable and quiet room where you can sit or lie down without distractions. Make sure you won't be interrupted during your meditation.

Step 2: Assume a comfortable position: Take a comfortable position with your spine straight and your feet flat on the ground. You may sit on a cushion or a chair, whatever feels comfortable for you.

Step 3: Take a deep breath: Take a few deep breaths in through your nose and out through your mouth. Allow your breath to become slow and deep. Concentrate on the feeling of air moving in and out of your body.

Step 4: Set your intention: As you inhale, set your intention to cultivate self-control. Visualise yourself breathing in self-control and breathing out impulsivity and lack of discipline.

Step 5: Visualise self-control: As you keep breathing, visualise self-control as a calm and steady energy that fills your body with composure and purpose. Imagine yourself being able to manage your emotions and behaviour in any situation.

Step 6: Repeat a positive affirmation: Repeat a positive affirmation to yourself, such as "I have the power to control my actions and reactions" or "I am disciplined and focused on achieving my goals". Say this affirmation with conviction and intention.

Step 7: Release tension: Scan your body for any areas of tension or discomfort and release them. If you detect any muscle tension, breathe into the sensation and allow it to dissolve.

Step 8: Take another deep breath: Take one final deep breath in through your nose and exhale slowly through your mouth. When you are ready, open your eyes and slowly return to the present moment.

Remember that you can perform this Breathing for Self-Control meditation whenever you need to cultivate more discipline and willpower in your life. It can help you develop greater self-awareness, resilience, and emotional regulation.

### Long Meditation

**30-40 minutes, or longer, daily or several times a week.**

**A Mindful Self-Control meditation, in which you focus on cultivating self-control in your life.**

An example of a powerful meditation to help embody self-control is the Mindful Self-Control Meditation. Here are the steps:

Step 1: Find a quiet and comfortable place: Start by finding a quiet and comfortable place where you can sit without being disturbed. You can sit cross-legged on a cushion or a chair, whichever feels more comfortable for you.

Step 2: Sit in a comfortable position: Sit in a comfortable position with your back straight and your feet flat on the ground. Place your hands on your lap or your knees, with your palms facing up or down.

Step 3: Take a few deep breaths: Take a few deep breaths in through your nose and out through your mouth. Allow your breath to become slow and deep. Focus on the sensation of air moving in and out of your body.

Step 4: Scan your body: Scan your body for any areas of tension or discomfort and release them. If you notice tension in your shoulders, for example, roll them back and down to release the tension.

Step 5: Set your intention: As you inhale, set your intention to cultivate self-control. Imagine that you are breathing in self-control and breathing out any negative thoughts or emotions that may hinder your ability to exercise self-control.

Step 6: Focus on your breath: Bring your attention to your breath and focus on the sensation of air moving in and out of your body. Allow your breath to become slow and steady.

Step 7: Observe your thoughts: As you continue to focus on your breath, notice any thoughts or emotions that arise. Observe them without judgment and allow them to pass without getting caught up in them.

Step 8: Bring your attention back to your breath: Whenever you find your mind wandering, bring your attention back to your breath. Allow your breath to serve as an anchor, bringing you back to the present moment.

Step 9: Repeat affirmations: Repeat affirmations to yourself that encourage self-control, such as "I am in control of my thoughts and emotions" or "I make wise and deliberate choices." Say these affirmations with sincerity and conviction.

Step 10: End with gratitude: When you are ready to end your meditation, take a few deep breaths and bring your attention back to your body. Take a moment to express gratitude for the practice and for yourself, and slowly open your eyes.

## Visualisation

**A short visualisation, practised at any time of the day, can be a powerful tool to shift your perspective.**

Imagine yourself standing in the centre of a storm, representing the chaos and turbulence of your thoughts and emotions. Visualise yourself taking deep, slow breaths, feeling centred and in control even during the storm.

## Affirmations

**Choose a single affirmation you are attracted to or several affirmations, and write them down or memorise them. You can add them to notes around the house. Pin them where you can see them. Chant them to yourself. Sing them. Start the day with some affirmations. Affirmations are a proven way to programme your subconscious, creating profound change.**

I am in control of my thoughts and actions.

I have the power to make choices that serve my best interests.

I am disciplined and focused on my goals.

I am patient and persistent in pursuing what I want.

I am mindful of my behaviour and make conscious choices.

I am strong in the face of temptation and adversity.

I am responsible for my own life and choices.

I am committed to living a healthy and balanced lifestyle.

I choose to delay gratification for long-term success.

I am capable of overcoming challenges and obstacles.

I am confident in my ability to make wise decisions.

I am self-aware and make choices that align with my values and principles.

Affirmations can be a powerful tool for cultivating self-control in our lives. By regularly repeating positive statements to ourselves, we can begin to shift our mindset and strengthen our ability to resist temptation and make conscious choices. When practising affirmations for self-control, we remind ourselves of our inner strength and commitment to our goals, which can help us stay on track even when faced with challenging situations.

Incorporating affirmations into our daily routine can also help us stay more mindful and present in the moment. When we pause to reflect on our intentions and repeat positive statements to ourselves, we bring our attention back to the present and focus on what we can control in our lives. This can help us let go of negative thoughts and emotions that can lead us astray and cultivate a sense of calm and inner peace. By consistently practising affirmations for self-control, we can build a stronger foundation for our self-discipline and create lasting positive change in our lives

---

Self-control is a crucial trait that can have a significant impact on our lives. It refers to our ability to regulate our thoughts, emotions, and behaviour, and make wise choices that align with our goals and values. Developing self-control takes time and practice, but it can lead to improved mental and emotional health, better relationships, and greater success in all areas of life. The process of learning to embody self-control involves cultivating self-awareness, setting clear intentions, and building healthy habits and routines that support our goals.

Self-control helps us to make better decisions and resist temptations that might otherwise lead us astray. By developing self-control, we can avoid impulsive actions that can harm ourselves and others, and instead make conscious choices that reflect our values and aspirations. This can lead to greater self-esteem, confidence, and fulfilment, as well as improved relationships with those around us. It can also help us to manage stress and overcome challenges with greater resilience and ease, allowing us to navigate life's ups and downs with greater grace and wisdom. Ultimately, embodying self-control can lead to a more fulfilling and purposeful life, and help us to realise our full potential as human beings.

全店営業中
歌舞伎町牧場
Mo-Mo-Paradise
FACE
コミック&ネットカフェ
comics & internet cafe
aprecio
アプレシオ
新宿最大
直進30m
ハイジアB1
ダーツ
ビリヤード&ダーツ
ゴルフ バグース
COPABOWL
まんが喫茶
ゲラゲラ
地域最大!!
ゲーム
メダル
クレーン
TVゲーム
カードゲーム
プリクラ
メンズサウナ
Pavilion
LUXOR Bar
RESTAURANT
コーヒー ショップ クール
無料案内所
カラ
まんが喫茶
GOD
麻雀
無料案内所
麺
ラッキー
B1
お好み焼
もんじゃ焼
味自慢
まつ里亭
B1
東京豚骨
らーめん
DINING BAR
OPEN

# THE LEGACY OF THE SAMURAI AND BUSHIDO

"The samurai and the idea of bushido are deeply ingrained in Japanese culture and have become a symbol of Japan's resilience and determination. Even today, these concepts inspire people to strive for excellence in all aspects of life, from business and education to sports and the arts….It's something that's timeless and can be applied to anybody's life." Tadashi Nakamura. Japanese-American filmmaker

The samurai class is one of Japan's most significant aspects of history, culture, and identity. Their legacy is one that has stood the test of time and continues to inspire people around the world. The samurai were warriors, philosophers, artists, and poets who embodied a unique way of life, emphasising loyalty, honour, courage, and discipline.

In modern Japan, the legacy of the samurai can be seen in various aspects of society. One of the most significant ways that the samurai's influence is celebrated is through the practice of traditional martial arts such as kendo and iaido. These martial arts were developed by the samurai and are still taught and practised today. Many Japanese people view these martial arts as a way to connect with their cultural heritage and learn valuable life skills such as discipline, focus, and perseverance.

In addition to martial arts, the samurai legacy is also celebrated through the annual celebration of Samurai Day, which takes place on February 14th. This holiday is a time for people to reflect on the samurai's history and accomplishments and honour their memory. Various events mark the day, including parades, exhibitions, and cultural performances.

The debate over the legacy of the samurai is one that has been ongoing in Japan for decades. It is not without controversy. On the one hand, some view the samurai as heroes, as symbols of honour, courage, and loyalty. They see the samurai as crucial to Japan's history and cultural identity. These people argue that the samurai were essential in maintaining social order during a time of significant political and social change in Japan. They see the samurai as a force for good who protected the weak and vulnerable from harm.

On the other hand, there are those who view the samurai as the oppressors of the common people. They argue that the samurai were a privileged class who used their power to maintain their own social and economic status at the expense of the lower classes. These people see the samurai as a relic of Japan's feudal past, an inherently unjust and oppressive system.

This debate is not just limited to older generations in Japan. Younger generations, too, have their own perspectives on the matter. For some, the samurai represent a bygone era that is interesting to study but has little relevance to modern Japan. Others, however, see the samurai as a source of inspiration, as exemplars of the values of discipline, courage, and loyalty.

It is important to note that these perspectives are not mutually exclusive. It is possible to acknowledge the role of the samurai in Japan's history while also recognising the injustices committed in their name. Similarly, it is possible to draw inspiration from the values of bushido without glorifying the violence and oppression that were also a part of the samurai legacy

Despite the debates, the samurai continue to inspire people in modern Japan. The values of bushido, such as loyalty, honour, and courage, are still admired by many and are seen as important ideals to strive for in daily life. These values are reflected in martial arts and various aspects of Japanese society, such as business, politics, and education.

The influence of the samurai is not limited to Japan. The samurai have gained significant popularity among Western audiences in recent years, with their stories and legends captivating people worldwide. Many films and TV series, such as "The Last Samurai" and "47 Ronin," have brought the samurai to the forefront of popular culture, showcasing their values and their way of life.

This global interest in samurai culture has led to increased tourism to Japan, as many visitors are eager to learn more about the country's rich history and traditions. In addition to visiting popular tourist destinations such as Tokyo and Kyoto, many tourists also visit historical sites such as samurai castles and battlefields to learn more about the samurai's way of life and their impact on Japanese history.

This increased interest in samurai culture has also led to a rise in the popularity of martial arts such as kendo and iaido, which the samurai developed. Many martial arts schools have opened in Western countries, allowing people to learn more about the samurai's way of life and their values. These martial arts are not just a form of physical exercise but also a way to connect with Japan's rich cultural heritage and to learn essential life skills such as discipline, focus, and perseverance.

Overall, the global interest in samurai culture is a testament to the enduring legacy of the samurai. While the samurai class officially ended with the Meiji Restoration in 1868, their influence on Japanese culture and society is still felt today, both within Japan and beyond. The samurai's values of discipline, honour, and courage continue to inspire people worldwide, and their legacy will undoubtedly continue to be celebrated and admired for many years to come.

The younger generation in Japan is a diverse group with a wide range of interests and perspectives. Many young people in Japan today are growing up in a very different world from the one their parents and grandparents experienced. Japan has become more Westernised in recent years, with many young people embracing Western fashion, music, and other cultural elements.

Despite this, many young people in Japan are still interested in traditional Japanese culture and history. Some of these young people are drawn to the samurai and their legacy, finding inspiration in their values and way of life.

For some, the draw of the samurai comes from the martial arts. Many young people in Japan practice traditional martial arts like kendo, judo, and karate. The samurai developed these martial arts in Japan, and they continue to be taught and practised today. For these young people, martial arts provide physical exercise, a sense of connection to their cultural heritage, and a way to learn important life skills like discipline, focus, and perseverance.

Others are more interested in the pop culture representations of the samurai, which can be found in anime, manga, and video games. These young people are drawn to the exciting and romanticised portrayals of samurai in popular media, with their stories of honour, courage, and sacrifice.

However, it is important to note that not all young people in Japan are interested in the samurai. Some see them as relics of the past, no longer relevant to modern society. Others view the samurai as symbols of Japan's imperialistic past and are critical of the way that they treated ordinary people.

Overall, the younger generation in Japan is a complex and diverse group, and it isn't easy to make sweeping generalisations about their attitudes towards the samurai. However, it is clear that many young people still find inspiration in the samurai and their legacy, whether through traditional martial arts or popular culture. The continued interest in the samurai among the younger generation is a testament to the enduring impact that these warriors have had on Japanese culture and society.

The legacy of the samurai is not just a matter of historical record; it remains an active, ongoing force in modern Japan and beyond. While it is true that there are different views on the samurai, ranging from reverence to criticism, the fact remains that the samurai continue to inspire and captivate people around the world. Their influence is evident in numerous aspects of contemporary culture, from martial arts to cinema, literature, and business.

One of the key reasons why the legacy of the samurai continues to endure is that their values and principles still resonate with people today. The tenets of bushido, such as loyalty, honour, and courage, are still highly regarded and admired by many, both in Japan and beyond. These principles offer a moral compass that can help guide individuals through life, and they are often seen as essential for success in a variety of fields, from sports to business.

In addition, the samurai are often viewed as symbols of Japan's unique cultural identity. While Japan has modernised and evolved in many ways, it has retained a strong sense of tradition and cultural heritage embodied in the samurai legacy. This cultural identity is seen as a source of pride and inspiration for Japanese people and those around the world drawn to Japanese culture.

Many industries in Japan have embraced the samurai legacy, including tourism, fashion, and technology. For example, there are numerous samurai-themed tourist attractions throughout Japan, from museums and historical sites to theme parks and restaurants. Fashion designers have also drawn inspiration from samurai armour and clothing, incorporating traditional motifs and designs into contemporary styles. In the world of technology, samurai-themed video games and other products have proven to be highly popular, further spreading awareness of samurai culture and values.

In recent years, the samurai have also inspired various technological advancements, particularly in the field of robotics. Japanese robotics engineers have created robots that are designed to emulate the movements and techniques of traditional samurai swordsmanship. These robots are not only a testament to the lasting legacy of the samurai, but they also represent Japan's cutting-edge technology and innovation.

George Lucas, the creator of Star Wars, has often spoken about how he was inspired by samurai culture when developing the Jedi Knights. The Jedi share many similarities with the samurai, including their code of honor, their mastery of a weapon (the lightsabre), and their disciplined lifestyle. Lucas has also cited the work of legendary Japanese filmmaker Akira Kurosawa as a significant influence on his vision for Star Wars. Kurosawa's films, such as Seven Samurai and Yojimbo, are classic examples of the samurai genre and were a major source of inspiration for the iconic lightsabre duels in Star Wars. In this way, the samurai legacy has not only influenced Japanese culture but has also left its mark on popular culture around the world.

Finally, the legacy of the samurai is a testament to the power of human resilience and adaptation. The samurai were able to thrive and succeed in a world that was constantly changing and evolving, adapting their skills and values to meet new challenges and circumstances. In doing so, they left behind a legacy that continues to inspire and guide people to this day.

In conclusion, the legacy of the samurai is complex and multifaceted, with both positive and negative aspects. However, by acknowledging the debates and having a nuanced understanding of the samurai's place in history, we can appreciate the significance of their legacy and the enduring impact that they have had on Japanese culture and society. The values and principles of bushido and the samurai's role in preserving Japan's cultural identity continue to inspire and captivate people in Japan and beyond. Their legacy is likely to endure for generations to come.

"The spirit of bushido is the embodiment of loyalty, courage, veracity, compassion, and honour. It is the power of the soul which overcomes all obstacles, the indomitable spirit of the warrior. It is moral courage and heroism, the love of truth and justice, the sense of duty and self-sacrifice. The samurai had no conception of a purely personal god, yet he was religious in the sense that he lived in the presence of the gods everywhere about him" - Nitobe Inazo

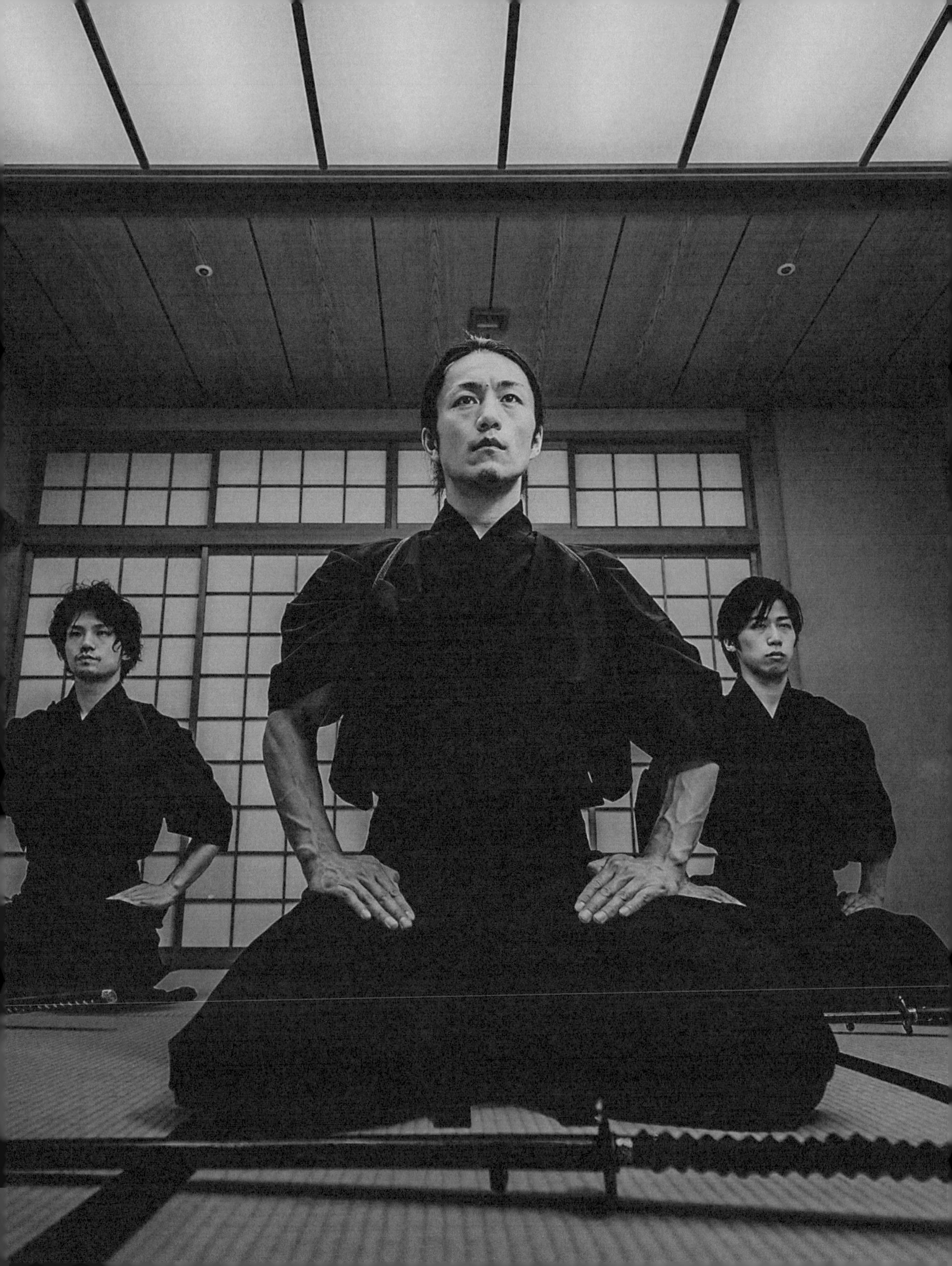

# CONCLUSION
## THE END....
## AND THE BEGINNING

In a world where self-help approaches are ubiquitous and often frustratingly superficial, Bushido offers a refreshing alternative. Despite being centuries old, this code of virtues and honour, developed among Japanese samurai, remains relevant and universal. While modern life may not involve the same physical dangers faced by samurai, it presents its own challenges that can be addressed through the wisdom and guidance of Bushido. By adopting even a few of its practices and embodying its eight virtues, anyone can find structure and strength to face the struggles of daily life. As humans, we all face doubts, insecurities, and stresses, but by taking action, no matter how small, we can begin to live the life of an Everyday Samurai.

Congratulations. You have made it to the end of The Everyday Samurai, and I hope I have been able to inspire you to at least consider adopting the Code of Bushido as your own personal code, if not to actually start working, day by day, at embodying the virtues of Bushido into your life.

In the 21st Century, we are bombarded with thousands of self-help approaches; everyone is a guru and has something to sell. I can't help feeling that most self-help gurus have never really put their own advice to use. It's just another industry looking to make a quick buck by developing the next big thing. Meanwhile, millions cry out for honest guidance and real hope. Millions are looking for a path, a lifestyle and a *way* that not only makes sense but embodies universal truths and wisdom.

There is nothing unique about Bushido. Certainly not in the way the self-help gurus would need it to be, to market it as the next big thing, which quickly becomes last month's disappointment. Bushido existed for centuries, if not a thousand years, before it was given its name. It existed as a collection of virtues, and an honour system, if you like, amongst men who lived hard lives, where death was a genuine possibility. It is not new. It's ancient. It's not unique. It's a codified collection of virtues that just make sense.

And perhaps *sense* is what we are looking for.

Have you tried any of the practices? Perhaps you have already developed a daily routine. Perhaps you are meditating whenever you get the chance. Maybe you are using the affirmations? Or perhaps you have started to pick and choose a few activities each week as a first step toward becoming an Everyday Samurai.

It's possible you are still thinking about it. That's fine too. Thinking about it is the start. No action occurs without us first thinking about it. Just don't think for too long.

Take action.

Any action. Massive imperfect action beats procrastination every time. Do something. Anything.

Do you feel like a Samurai yet?

What does a Samurai feel like?

We live relatively comfortable lives here in the 21st century. We aren't warriors. Or at least most of us aren't warriors. We still live in a society where warriors are needed, and we can be thankful some step forward to play that role. For the rest of us, our battleground is daily life.

Work

Relationships

Our own minds and emotions

That's where the real battles take place.

Kids fight. But for men and women, the real fight is in paying the bills, keeping a roof over our heads, feeding ourselves and our families, raising children to the very best of our abilities to be the very best they can be, and all while being conscious and loving parents, partners and members of society.

The Samurai had complicated lives. And those lives were often cut short in the most brutal fashion imaginable. For most of us, that is a far cry from what we know and experience. The Samurai adopted Bushido because it made sense to them and offered a moral framework and context for them to live their best lives, no matter how short and violent they might be. Bushido worked for them because universal truths are….universal. They work. And they never stop working.

While our lives are not based on violence and death, you and I have profound challenges. Living in the 21st century isn't easy. For all our technology, healthcare, education and social structures, it still comes down to paying the rent and feeding ourselves. The enormous rise in social unrest and discontent, mental and emotional illnesses and the threats of climate change, war and financial collapse means we are all under stress and looking for anything to give us structure and context.

Bushido can do that.

It might not be the answer to everything.

But Bushido can give you structure and strength. But by working diligently and with focus and discipline, even for just ten minutes a day, the changes will start to come into your life. Bushido has something to offer all of us, no matter what we perceive our weaknesses to be or what areas of our lives need help. The eight virtues cover all the bases.

Why?

Because humans never change. Whether we are feudal lords, leading armies of samurai into battle, whether we are single parents raising children on a limited budget, whether we are students, or whether we are stuck in an office job while dreaming of becoming rock stars, we still suffer the same doubts, insecurities and stresses. We are all human, and our brains are hardwired over millions of years to function and react similarly. Over and over again.

Have you ever laid awake at night and worried? So did every Samurai that ever lived.

Have you ever felt insecure over a relationship? So did every Samurai.

Have you ever reacted badly and then run it over in your mind a thousand times, wishing you had said or done it differently?

Yes, so did every Samurai.

We may not practice with the sword for hours every day and fight to the death over points of honour. But we are closer to those men and women than we realise. Put them in a suit and let them work in our office for a week, or let them try to entertain our children during the school holidays, or balance a budget for a family when food prices are rising every month, and we will see they are no different to us.

We all need help.

And Bushido, amongst many self-help systems and questionable ideas, is a system that works. We know because the samurai based their lives on it.

It gives us help and provides a framework and context for coping with every conflict, every insecurity and every problem that might slip into our lives.

The Eight Virtues of Bushido will change your life. But only if you allow it to change your life. And to allow it, you must make that commitment to change. We can all be better. We can all create change that will benefit ourselves, our families and our society. And if every one of us committed to change, our world would quickly become the place we all want it to be rather than the place it is becoming.

Whenever I struggle to start on something, I always tell myself to do the things now that my future self will thank me for. And I look ahead, a year or two, and imagine where I could be and what I might have achieved. And then, I take the first step.

So do something today that your future self will thank you for. Do something today that will bring you one step closer to living your best life. And tomorrow, take another step, and another and another. One step at a time until you have become the person you want to be.

Start adopting the virtues of Bushido into your life.

More importantly, start to embody those virtues. Take the advice for each virtue, and gently apply it to each aspect of your life. Use the meditations and affirmations too. Make it a daily practice. Ten minutes a day is all it takes for change to start happening, and as you change, you'll find it easier and easier to create more change. The effects will multiply and snowball.

The premise of The Everyday Samurai is that by adopting the Bushido code and embodying the eight virtues, we can all become Samurai. We can all take on the spirit of the samurai

We can all become Everyday Samurai

I firmly believe this is a realistic goal for everyone.

We are all works in progress. We are all growing and evolving, facing the challenges and stresses of our lives, and doing our best to muddle through. I am no different to you. But I have made a firm commitment to adopt the Eight Virtues and work towards being the best version of myself that I can be for my family, my relationships and my society.

So I invite you to do the same.

Join me, and become an Everyday Samurai.

Let's raise an army of Everyday Samurai and fight against the systems, judgements and challenges that drag us down and away from our dreams and destinies.

We can do this.

Inside you is an ancient warrior ready to face the future fearlessly and with courage, wisdom and determination.

YOU *are* the Everyday Samurai.

Let's do it.

| 献燈 交野市 金剛迪子 | 献燈 京都市 福西勇夫 | 献燈 京都市 中川勝夫 | 献燈 八幡市 寺田 勤 | 献燈 西京極幼稚園 園長 三浦俊良 | 献燈 西京極幼稚園 園長 三浦俊良 | 献燈 西京極幼稚園 園長 三浦俊良 |
|---|---|---|---|---|---|---|
| 献燈 町田市 佐藤恵美 | 献燈 京都市 川崎忠男 | 献燈 倉敷市 沼本克明 | 献燈 京都市 八集堂印刷社 | 献燈 西京極幼稚園 教職員一同 | 献燈 西京極幼稚園 教職員一同 | 献燈 西京極幼稚園 教職員一同 |
| 献燈 横浜市 村山祐輔 | 献燈 (株)コンプレ 松本吉弘 | 献燈 長岡京市 東口次朗 | 献燈 (有)京都市 田辺建築塗装 | 献燈 京都市 宇野 治 | 献燈 中央美術(有) 末吉徳祐 | 献燈 舞妓焼 志垣吉昭 |

# REFERENCES AND FURTHER READING

**Hagakure: The Book of the Samurai by Yamamoto Tsunetomo** - This classic text is a collection of teachings and reflections on the samurai way of life, including their code of conduct, rituals, and philosophy.

**Bushido: The Soul of Japan by Inazo Nitobe** - First published in 1900, this book comprehensively explores the Bushido code and its role in shaping Japanese culture and society.

**The Samurai: A Military History by Stephen Turnbull** provides a detailed history of the samurai class, from their origins in feudal Japan to their ultimate decline in the 19th century.

**The Book of Five Rings by Miyamoto Musashi** - A classic text on samurai strategy and philosophy, "The Book of Five Rings" offers insights into the mindset and tactics of the samurai warrior.

**The Samurai Swordsman: Master of War by Stephen Turnbull** - This book focuses on the art of swordsmanship and its importance to the samurai warrior, with a particular emphasis on the famous samurai swordsman Miyamoto Musashi.

**Autumn Lightning: The Education of an American Samurai by Dave Lowry** - This personal memoir explores the author's journey to master the art of the samurai sword and his insights into the philosophy and lifestyle of the samurai warrior.

**Samurai: An Illustrated History by Mitsuo** Kure - This visually stunning book provides a comprehensive overview of the samurai class, from their clothing and weapons to their role in Japanese society and culture

**The Code of the Samurai: A Modern Translation of the Bushido Shoshinshu of Taira Shigesuke by Oscar Ratti and Adele Westbrook** - This book provides a modern translation of a classic text on the Bushido code, offering insights into the values and principles that guided the samurai way of life.

**The Sword and the Mind by Yagyu Munenori** explores the relationship between swordsmanship and Zen Buddhism, providing insights into the spiritual and philosophical dimensions of the samurai warrior's training.

**The Samurai Spirit: Ancient Wisdom for Modern Life by Inazo Nitobe** - This book explores the relevance of the samurai code of conduct to modern life, offering insights into how the principles of Bushido can be applied to contemporary challenges.

**The Book of Samurai: The Collected Teachings of Yamamoto Tsunetomo by William Scott Wilson** provides a comprehensive collection of teachings from Yamamoto Tsunetomo's "Hagakure," offering insights into the samurai warrior's way of life.

**The Way of the Samurai: Yukio Mishima on Hagakure in Modern Life edited by Kathryn Sparling** - This book features a collection of essays by the famous Japanese author Yukio Mishima, offering his reflections on the samurai code of conduct and its relevance to modern life

**The Way of the Samurai: The Legacy of Japan's Warrior Heroes by Carol Gaskin and Vince Matsuda** explores the history, philosophy, and legacy of the samurai warrior class, including their code of conduct and martial arts. The book features photographs, artwork, and quotes from samurai writings, providing a comprehensive overview of the samurai way of life and its relevance to modern times.

**The Book of Samurai: Book One: The Fundamental Teachings by Antony Cummins** - This book provides a comprehensive overview of the fundamental teachings of the samurai, including their code of conduct, martial arts, and spiritual practices.

**Samurai Women: 1184-1877 by Stephen Turnbull** - This book explores the lives and roles of women within the samurai class, offering a unique perspective on the samurai warrior's way of life.

**The Lone Samurai: The Life of Miyamoto Musashi by William Scott Wilson** - This biography provides a detailed account of the life and achievements of the famous samurai swordsman Miyamoto Musashi, offering insights into his martial arts philosophy and techniques.

**The Samurai and the Sacred: The Path of the Warrior by Stephen Turnbull** explores the samurai class's spiritual and religious beliefs, including their relationship with Zen Buddhism and Shintoism.

**Bushido: The Way of the Samurai by Tsunetomo Yamamoto, Miyamoto Musashi, and Yamaga Soko** - This book is a collection of three classic texts on the Bushido code, providing a broad overview of the values and principles that guided the samurai warrior's way of life.

**Samurai Code: The 7 Virtues of Bushido and the Samurai Creed by Boye Lafayette De Mente** explores the seven virtues of Bushido and how they can be applied to modern life, providing insights into the enduring relevance of the samurai code of conduct.

**Zen and Japanese Culture by D.T. Suzuki** - This classic text explores the relationship between Zen Buddhism and Japanese culture, including the influence of Zen on art, architecture, and aesthetics.

**Zen Mind, Beginner's Mind by Shunryu Suzuki** - This book introduces Zen Buddhism and its teachings, focusing on the importance of cultivating a beginner's mind in one's spiritual practice.

**The Complete Guide to Zen Meditation by Koshin Paley Ellison** - This guide provides practical advice and guidance on starting a Zen meditation practice, including instructions on posture, breath, and mindfulness.

**Zen in the Art of Archery by Eugen Herrigel** - This book explores the connection between Zen Buddhism and the practice of archery, offering insights into the role of mindfulness and intuition in the pursuit of mastery.

**Zen and the Samurai by D.T. Suzuki** - This book examines the influence of Zen Buddhism on the samurai way of life, including the role of meditation and mindfulness in the samurai warrior's training and philosophy.

**Zen in the Martial Arts by Joe Hyams** - This book explores the connection between Zen Buddhism and the martial arts, including insights into the mindset and training of the martial artist.

**Zen and Japanese Culture: Selected Essays by D.T. Suzuki** - This collection of essays by D.T. Suzuki explores various aspects of Zen Buddhism and its influence on Japanese culture, including topics such as aesthetics, ethics, and social philosophy.

**The Essence of Zen: The Teachings of Sekkei Harada by Sekkei Harada** - This book provides a comprehensive overview of Zen Buddhism and its teachings, with a particular focus on the importance of mindfulness and meditation in daily life.

**The Way of Zen by Alan Watts** - This classic text offers an introduction to Zen Buddhism and its teachings, with a focus on the role of intuition and direct experience in spiritual practice.

**Zen and the Art of Motorcycle Maintenance** by Robert M. Pirsig - This philosophical work explores the relationship between Zen Buddhism and the pursuit of excellence in one's chosen field, with a particular focus on the art of motorcycle maintenance.

**The Wabi-Sabi House: The Japanese Art of Imperfect Beauty by Robyn Griggs Lawrence** explores the Japanese aesthetic philosophy of wabi-sabi, which embraces imperfection, transience, and simplicity. The book offers practical advice on incorporating wabi-sabi into home design and daily life, highlighting the beauty and authenticity of imperfections and natural materials.

**Budo: The Art of Killing** directed by Masayoshi Nemoto and produced by Hisao Masuda is a documentary film that explores the history and philosophy of Japanese martial arts and their evolution into modern self-defence techniques. The film features martial arts masters and practitioners, as well as demonstrations of various martial arts styles and techniques. The title is unfortunate, and misrepresents the film, which focuses on the beauty and skill of the traditional arts. Stylish and atmospheric. Highly recommended.

Made in United States
Troutdale, OR
02/22/2025